Ziva Kronzon: Embers

Gideon Ofrat

The book is published in conjunction with Ziva Kronzon's retrospective exhibition at the Zhou B Art Center in Chicago, April-May 2007

Ziva Kronzon: Embers

Edited by Gideon Ofrat

Design and Production: Magen Halutz
English Translation: Peretz Kidron
Hebrew and English Text Editing: Einat Adi
Graphics: Alva Halutz
Photography: James Dee, Avraham Hay, Eytan Kaufman, Shira Kronzon,
                        Wolfgang J. Popp, A. Vegenfeld
Archive Photography: Lili Sheer
Digital processing: Kiril Zotov

Dimensions are given in centimeters, height x width x depth

Front cover: *Bucket*, from *Dispersion*, 1993 [see p. 198]
Back cover: *Container*, 1986 [see p. 281]

Ziva Kronzon: Embers

To Yehoshua Shisha-Halevy, who never got to cast the bomb-shelter roof.

To my children: Iris and Ori; Rafi and Elisa; Shira and David; Ella, Adam and Lucy

Acknowledgements

To my distant yet very close friends and family – my life support,
To Itzhak Kronzon, who has made a home for me,
To Buky Schwartz, who removed obstacles at the start of the road,
And to Gideon Ofrat who has held my hand.

Special thanks to Dan Miron for his help.

Table of Contents

Ziva Kronzon   Foreword   9

Oskar Friedl   As Long as the Frogs are Croaking   13

Gideon Ofrat   Embers   15

     Introduction: Fire and Embers   15

     Kiryat Haim, 1948: Glowing Coal   19

     Jerusalem, Bezalel, 1955-1959   27

     Tel Aviv, Illustrations, 1960-1971   35

     Drawings for Stories by Kafka, Agnon, and Others [Works]   57

     New York, Etchings, 1973-1978   69

     Etchings: Sheets and Containers [Works]   81

     Towards "Blind Drawings," 1978-1981   87

     "Incas' Chronicles," 1981-1983   119

     From Collagraphs to Containers, 1983-1985   141

     Archive Fever   151

     Between Hades and Hephaestus, 1990-1991   185

     The Burden of Time, The Burden of Space   245

     Slain upon her High Places   253

     Art and War   271

     "Dispersion," 1994   289

     "Terra Interdicta," 1994-2001   311

     "Night Vision," 2002   337

     "Gleaning," 2005   359

     Days of Commemoration, Days of Destruction   373

     To Date   381

     Retrospective [Works]   389

Biographical Notes   397

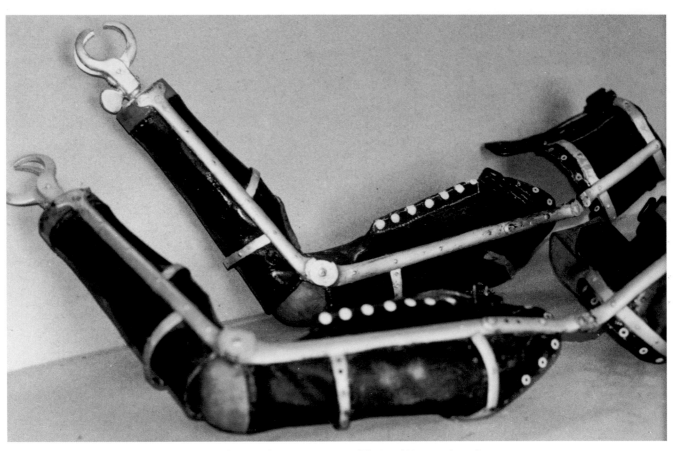

The Hero's Two Right Hands, 1994, color photograph, 11x19, courtesy of The Israel Museum, Jerusalem

Foreword

Ziva Kronzon

"Once upon a time there was a King, and the King had a daughter…"

Almost half a century ago, while serving my military duty in the IDF, I had to do some moonlighting jobs in order to pay back the loan which was given to me by the Defense Ministry office for the support of bereaved families. That office had helped in paying my education expenses throughout my studies at the Bezalel School of Arts and Crafts, which later became the Bezalel Academy of Art and Design. After my graduation I was drafted to the IDF and stationed at the publishing house of Ma'arachot – The official IDF monthly publication. These offices were located in an old stone house which was built at the end of the 19th century by the German Templars who settled in the Holy Land. There, I met NCO (and later Doctor and Professor) Adir Cohen, and drew, for an extra fee, hundreds of illustrations for the folk tales which he collected, translated and edited, to be published at the M. Mizrahi civilian publishing house in Tel Aviv.

Of all the characters created by my drawing pencil, the only one I vividly recall is the daughter of the aforementioned King, who intended to marry her to a prince. But the beautiful princess resisted his plans and insisted, instead, on marrying her beloved – a young commoner. The King, realizing his daughter's stubbornness, agreed to let her have her way, on one condition: that she would show up at a certain time and place,

> Riding but not riding
>
> Dressed but not dressed
>
> And carrying a present which is not a present

A Paradox!

Now, nearly fifty years later, advancing backwards – with my back towards the ever shrinking future and my face towards the ever growing past – I keep carrying my personal memories and the idea of the paradox as the essence of our life. Throughout my artistic work I have tried to express our paradoxical existence in a metaphorical way, and the perspective I have gained with time allows me to describe fragments of those attempts.

In 1972, when I came to New York, I started to create what is called "fine art," rather than "low" applied art. Following my experience as an illustrator in Israel, I was drawn to work on paper, to the printing process and "replication," and decided accordingly to study the techniques of artistic printmaking. I created series of etchings in several techniques. Preparing the metal plates and manipulating the manual iron printing press entailed a physical struggle. Seven years of hard work convinced me that this time-consuming technical hardship hindered my galloping creative visions, and I therefore shifted my focus to a different medium – the monoprint, which enabled me to materialize my artistic ideas at a more satisfactory pace. Gradually, details were omitted and my palette became more and more minimal, until all trace of color had disappeared from my works. Thus I came to represent the notion of the paradox in a series called "Blind Drawings."

These "drawings" were not drawings, and the "blindness" was not blind. I "drew" them by deeply embossing the paper with a heavy printing press. Out of this series, and as an integral part of it, grew the "Incas' Chronicles" works – a series that tells the history of the Inca in a paradoxical way. I found that history and the secret of the Inca Empire comparable in many aspects to the history of my homeland, the State of Israel. I documented on paper, in contemporary terms and idioms, fictitious events of a nation that had no knowledge of paper or writing, and therefore had limited capacity for documentation. Thus I found a *tabula rasa* for my personal projections; for the paradoxical games and the sculptural qualities made possible by working with paper as a medium.

In 1982, soon after the end of the first Lebanon War, I started to combine paper and metal, joining and juxtaposing them in order to stress their opposing qualities. My works had become three-dimensional. I created my first reliquaries – originally containers for the preservation of relics of Christian Saints, my reliquaries were perishable. I saw them as "perishable memorials," elaborating on the notion of paradox while calling for the preservation of life instead of the perpetuation of death.

These metal-like paper structures grew in size and became modular. Their design and color gave them a metallic appearance, projecting power and stability which were in fact illusory, as they were made of a vulnerable and ephemeral material. I jotted down at the time: "By building deceptive retreats and nonfunctional, symbolic defense systems in the face of violent reality, I am trying to reflect the absurdity of our existence." I dealt with the damaged and distorted, the incomplete, atrophied and perishable, the ephemeral, the process of continuous change, always aware of the Heraclitean paradox – namely, that the only stable state is everlasting change.

At the time, I associated my "metal" structures with the Jews' need for lightweight luggage in their endless wandering, and with Shimon Dubnow's hypothesis that the Jewish people's survival was made possible due to its capacity for wandering. And I wonder: would staying-put in one place lead a people to a reverse result?

The cast paper items that I created were purposely disfigured while manufacturing them, so that they were both finished products and flawed "rejects" from the start, thus acquiring a new identity, deceitful at times – as if proving Kurt Schwitters' statement: "Everything is true – and also the complete opposite." The installations I composed with these deceptive paper structures were like charred, eroded phantoms left behind in a battlefield.

In 1994 I exhibited at the Nelly Aman Gallery in Tel Aviv an installation named *Dispersion*. It was a large floor installation containing dispersed objects cast in paper as well as found objects, some of them rectified; that is, original objects, possibly matrices – the origins of the simulation. The show presented a dystopic microcosm reflecting a personal reality.

At the same time, beginning in 1992, I photographed numerous, mostly quite mundane surroundings, finding a common denominator in them – a collective title. I thought I would call them "Infrared," but then my friend Gideon Ofrat suggested "Night Vision." Under that name I have gathered analog and digital photographs, on which I keep on working to this day. In the leaflet that accompanied the show I highlighted once again the concept of the paradox: "This is a deceptive show: the photos were not taken with an Infrared camera which exposes details invisible to the ordinary eye – although that is their pretense…'Night Vision' depicts objects exposed to a different light, observed in a different light – their appearance distorted, enigmatic, false and elusive. Their identity is an illusion. They represent a state of mind rather than what the eye perceives."

In 2004 I created another floor installation. I meant to call it "Fresh Water? Well? Life?" but, once again on Gideon Ofrat's suggestion, I called it by the wonderful title "Gleaning." This work combines gleaned objects and works done by me over the last forty years. It deals with time, memory and paradox. While working on it I thought about Penelope, Odysseus' wife, who weaved and unweaved, weaved and unweaved in order to delay her suitors, and I wondered: did she spend her entire life on this paradoxical activity of doing and undoing? Do I, "playing seriously" with my artwork, do so because the physical, material activity provides me with a sense of control over the chaos around me?

Lest I forget: "…the King's beautiful daughter appeared in front of her father at the designated time and place, mounted on a donkey but with her feet touching the ground, wearing a dress made of a fishnet, and holding in her palms a white dove which flew away when she handed it over to her father. The princess thus succeeded in overcoming the paradox and happily married her sweetheart."

That's how it is in fairytales.

As Long as the Frogs are Croaking

Oskar Friedl

The Zhou B Art Center is honored to host Ziva Kronzon's retrospective exhibition, which culminates her life-long artistic journey. Kronzon's installations use a variety of media to reflect on incidents of global significance by engaging the consciousness and the sensory levels of the viewer in a synthesis of environmental and political awareness.

Kronzon's sculptures and installations mirror the decay and prosperity of the environment, portraying uncertainty by questioning and doubting what is often taken for granted as a logical part of reality. She acts as an environmental historian, tracking and logging the changes which surround her. Ziva Kronzon is an artist who lives in two worlds, traveling freely between two distinct societies, and her works have depicted the destruction in war-torn Israel as well as the terror and ruin in New York. She succeeds in linking both cultures in her installations, while alluding to the affluence at the basis of these two harsh environments.

In her work from 1995, *Cluster*, Kronzon uses the frog as an analogy of a traveler between worlds; for her, these two worlds are Israel and the United States. Just like an amphibian, she depends on two worlds for her survival and therefore keeps a watchful eye on both. As reviewed by Gideon Ofrat, the frog has had many historical interpretations; to these I would like to add its presence as an indicator of a healthy environment. The frog is an alarm bell that indicates the cleanness of the water and the cohesive nature of the environment. The artist Ziva Kronson is just as indicative of a culture's capacity to hold together regardless of the destruction it is facing.

I have known Kronzon's work for many years and am greatly impressed by her ability to create a cultural dialogue and interpret the environmental climate through art. Not only does Kronzon act as an indicator of environmental affluence, but her works themselves reflect the aseptic core from which we prosper. As long as the frog continues to croak, the water that we drink and of which we are made remains untainted. Kronzon provides hope amidst the dismay in the two cultures she weds in both her life and art.

Ziva Kronzon in her New York studio, 1996

Embers

Gideon Ofrat

Introduction: Fire and Embers

Thirty four years have elapsed since Ziva Kronzon's arrival in New York from Tel Aviv. It was 1972, the golden age of conceptual art in the USA and Europe, and the 33-year-old graphic designer, popular in Israel as a delightful illustrator of books for young people, launched upon a long and convoluted – though remarkably consistent – artistic course, which would take her all the way from surrealist etchings, by way of post-minimalist objects, to pluralist installations verging on entropy, if not downright chaos.

Residence in Manhattan (after three years, 1972-75, of a demanding and uncomfortable sojourn in the Bronx) immersed the artist in the dynamic artistic abundance of museums and galleries in a city at the cutting edge of global avant-garde. Kronzon, curious and avid for knowledge, did not remain passive. On the contrary: with seemingly insatiable cultural appetite, she set about devouring the dizzying artistic offerings, learning and ingesting, casting off the residues of applied graphics implanted in her in the "New Bezalel" school of Arts and Crafts in the late fifties. Against this New York setting, Ziva Kronzon would experience artistic rebirth, cutting the umbilical cord that still bound her to the friendly and gracious sketches by Yossi Stern, a venerated "New Bezalel" teacher, while increasingly turning to the painful materials buried within her psyche for decades. Possibly the very distance from Israel facilitated her artistic tackling of that blazing deposit, that living, blistering ember originating in her childhood.

At the same time, the Kronzons, well aware of the existential paradox, transformed their New York apartment into an Israeli preserve. "I'm the most Israeli thing that exists," Kronzon told a journalist in 2002,[1] adding: "To this day, I feel at home in Tel Aviv. In the United States, I'm a stranger." Indeed, over

1   David Rapp, "She Sees in the Dark," *Haaretz*, 17 June 2002 [Hebrew].

decades, Ziva and Itzhak Kronzon (a world-renowned cardiology professor, as well as a witty, sensitive writer) have kept up daily contact with Israel: following Israeli media, daily phone calls to friends and relatives in Israel, regularly hosting Israeli friends, building a home in Israel and paying frequent visits there. In other words: their Israeli existence has in no way diminished through their relocation to the United States, which started out with a plan for a temporary sojourn and ended up with a permanent home. "As absurd as it is, that's my life, and it's a great life. My emotional roots and my beliefs are a result of being Israeli. I feed on my longings for Israel. Longing is an integral part of my life, I need it."[2]

2   Assi Weinstein, "Articulating the Absurd," *Atmosphere*, 15 September 2005.

It is not a case of sentimental pangs of exile; rather, it is one of yearning for a utopian sense of home, underpinned by destruction. It was precisely this remoteness in time and space from the scenes of her childhood and adolescence that has intensified for Kronzon residues of her early childhood in Kiryat Haim – residues enveloped in the cobwebs of time, of Israeli anxieties and a Jewish-Israeli history of war and sacrifice. From this "cocoon," which we shall encounter later, Kronzon's new art emerged – art sustained and fed by a core experience that is personal and Israeli, but adopting forms and materials in the spirit of contemporary Western art, which the artist attained in her own authentic, consistent way.

This Israeli-American dualism did not escape some of the more important writers about Kronzon's work. In 1991, Donald Kuspit, who was to write no less than four catalogue essays on her work, observed the duality in images of Israeli potency set against a fundamental Israeli vulnerability stemming from the trauma of the Holocaust. But in pointing out the expressive minimalism in the artist's syntax, he also set her within a central movement of contemporary American art.

The chapters to follow will trace this dualism of content and form. They will lead the reader through contemporary artistic languages familiar with Duchamp's readymade and minimalist serialism, languages that also remember American Pop art and Josef Beuys' installations, as well as the triumph of photography towards the end of the millennium. But in the depths of these ramified languages there has been a consistent glow of personal semantics, if only as the burning ember of a personal calamity translated into humanist trepidation; the ember that imbues Kronzon's work with its power and uniqueness.

"Embers," the book is called – and the equivalent Hebrew term, *remetz*, denotes not only hot cinders with remaining sparks of fire, but also a square grid. Like warm cinders, it is the memory of all-consuming fire, the historical as well as the artist's personal flame of the Holocaust (*holókaustos* = burned whole). Like hot cinders, it is still dangerous, still bearing within it burning coals that sear anyone delving into them. And like hot cinders, it is a great disintegration, the utter fragmentation whose formal echoes we shall detect throughout Kronzon's work. But at the same time, the *remetz* of the square grid is an act of structuring in geometrical squares, an anesthetization of the catastrophe, geometrical minimalism that counterbalances the chaos in Kronzon's work, endowing it with an affirmation of life. This too will be considered in the chapters to come.

Ziva Kronzon, New York, 1972

Yehoshua Shisha-Halevi (kneeling on the right) and friends, last photograph, 1948

Kiryat Haim, 1948: Glowing Coal

The modest cube-shaped house stands on Aleph Street, the first street in Kiryat Haim, close to the sand dunes and railway track. Running parallel to it to the east are other streets named for the letters of the Hebrew alphabet: Bet, Gimel etc. It is Friday, the month of July, a hot summer during which the humidity does not let up even when evening descends upon the houses near the sand dunes. Nine-year-old Ziva is standing on the broad front terrace. A truck approaches the house. It halts and Dad's army colleague steps down. A military operation is planned for tonight. Dad comes out on the terrace, in uniform, gun in hand, a helmet on his head. He kneels beside his little girl, kisses her warmly and leaves. Ziva watches him stride along the path to the gate and go out into the street. The truck vanishes into the darkness.

Saturday morning. Shabbath finery, a story book. At noon she joins her mother, along with her two-year-old baby brother, for a visit to friends, Viennese-born like Mom. After tea and cakes, on their way back through the deserted streets, Ziva and her mother reach Kiryat Haim's "main street." The sun still beats down. Between Gimel and Dalet streets, Mom halts abruptly, turns and mutters something to herself. Ziva too notices a man with two small children clasped in his hands half a block away. She knows the man: he is a soldier from Dad's squadron, who came with the others to summon him the evening before. He too recognizes Mom. He notices her, turns his back on her and hastens away with his children. At that moment, Ziva realizes that "it's bad." Mom hastens her steps and proceeds home on Aleph Street. Mom can scarcely speak Hebrew, she has no close friends and there is no phone. Evening descends.

Ziva recalls, in a flash, her mother striding back and forth in the middle of the night, still dressed. A fleeting image that is seared deep in her memory. "Apparently, that was the moment of awareness of loss," she will say years later.[3]

On Sunday, late morning, uncle Malachi arrived with the news. Later, on the path leading from the gate to the house, down a couple of steps, a short sentence from her overwhelmed mother, something like "Never mind, Dad

3   All unreferenced quotations
     of Ziva Kronzon are from
     conversations with the author.

Planting a wood in memory of Yehoshua Shisha-Halevi, in Western Galilee, 1949

fell for our homeland." Later that day uncle Eitan arrived from Kibbutz Sarid. Uncle Yigael, from Kibbutz Bet Ha'arava, was cut off in Sodom with other kibbutz members. Ziva remained in the neighbors' yard. She climbed a tree and swung on its branches. Curious questions were asked, and Ziva said she'd known all along.

That night she took a notebook and pencil and wrote rhymed poems. "Poems of blood, sweat and tears," she was to describe them ironically much later. In time, she realized that in the course of that single night she had undergone a sharp change, a transformation into who she is to this day. Fifty years later, she concludes: "It was a revelation of Self. A maturation process in hours – and I know that I've survived, ever since, by means of art."

A month or so after her father's death in the 1948 War, the most significant and constitutive event of Ziva Kronzon's life – "I'm a veteran among War of Independence orphans," she says ironically – the family moved from Kiryat Haim into the city of Haifa. Ziva's mother, as mentioned, had been born into a comfortable bourgeois family in Vienna. Her father, born in Ottoman Palestine, was, on his mother's side, a scion of the Stampfer family, pioneers, founders of the first Zionist settlement in the Holy Land, Petach Tikva. On his own father's side, he came from an Austrian family with Spanish roots, among the thirteenth century founders of the city of Mattersburg. In Palestine, Ziva's father had been a member of the labor youth movement Hanoar Ha'oved, going on to join the more radical Bahrut Sotzialistit ("Socialist Youth"). He was employed as a skilled mechanic at the Shemen factory in the Haifa bay area, carrying home the Socialist élan so predominant at the time in Kiryat Haim and the city commonly referred to as "Red Haifa."

When the family moved to Haifa, Ziva discovered that the Israeli national anthem was Hatikva, not L'Internationale. By now, little Ziva was aware of four men of her close family who had fallen in the 1948 War. Years later, she would say: "The myth of the sacrifice of Isaac had become my own personal story," adding, on the subject of war in general: "It is violence vindicated by the brandishing of flags."[4] In Voltaire's *Candide* she finds an apt description of war – and of her own stance in relation to it:

4   Rivka Raz, "Where was Sarah at the Sacrifice of Isaac?" *Yedioth Ahronoth*, *Z'manim Modernim* supplement, 3 May 1989 [Hebrew].

New growth on old Tamarisk trees after massive pruning, opposite Ziva's Kiryat Haim home, 1948
Oil on cardboard, 23x28 (painted at age 9)

Those who have never seen two well-trained armies drawn up for battle, can have no idea of the beauty and brilliance of the display. Bugles, fifes, oboes, drums, and salvoes of artillery produced such a harmony as Hell itself could not rival. The opening barrage destroyed about six thousand men on each side. Rifle-fire which followed rid this best of worlds of about nine or ten thousand villains who infested its surface. Finally, the bayonet provided 'sufficient reason' for the death of several thousand more. The total casualties amounted to about thirty thousand. Candide trembled like a philosopher, and hid himself as best he could during this heroic butchery. [5]

5   Voltaire, *Candide: Or Optimism*, translated by John Butt, Penguin Classics, 1950, pp. 25.

In the introduction to the catalogue of her 1995 exhibition at the Nelly Aman gallery in Tel Aviv, Donald Kuspit affirmed: "More than most, Ziva Kronzon's works of art are symptoms of disaster, residues of agony. They are *memento mori* of her experience of war, and more broadly, 'statements' about the inevitability of violence."[6] Later, speaking on the subject of war in a 2002 interview to an Israeli journalist, Kronzon may have been describing her own hollow, non-functional works, so misleading in their external appearance: "In my perception, war is non-functional action, empty of content, mendacious and destructive." Later, she admitted: "I've been in the shadow of violent death all my life, and it is precisely because I have suffered directly from it that I can't stand what often appears to me like a general national celebration of death. The numerous monuments in Israel remind me of the Christian cult of relics. It's a paradoxical attempt to preserve something that's gone."[7]

6   Donald Kuspit, cat. *Ziva Kronzon*, Nelly Aman gallery, Tel Aviv, 1995.

7   See footnote 1.

Years later, in the catalogue for her exhibition at the gallery of the Makor Jewish cultural center in New York, Kronzon related:

I was born in Eretz Israel to a family of pioneers. My forebears there had witnessed the rise and the fall of the Ottoman Empire and the coming and going of the British. My family history, and my personal experience of growing up in a place torn by violence, where one must adapt daily in order to survive, taught me to encounter the theater of transition and to accept the notion that only the beginning and the end are set milestones, while the road between is constantly changing.

Ten years previously, she wrote:

The tense axis stretching between the offending polarity and the offended polarity is my playground. The axis is constructed of points of encounter between these polarities, opposing and clutching one another, and each point of encounter is charged with destructive energy – that repeatedly destroys the extant, which is repeatedly re-created to be destroyed again. My work is preoccupied with documentation of the endless dynamic between life and death, growth and extinction.[8]

8   From the artist's archive, New York.

In 1993, Kronzon scattered on the floor of her studio numerous objects she had accumulated in her storeroom. Among them she came upon an iron wire mesh that she rolled up into a cylinder, upon which she hung a photograph of her father in battledress. The photograph too was found in her storeroom. At the conceptual level, each of Kronzon's works is imprinted with her father's image. And each work seems to expand the detailed list: weaponry, cartridge belt with bullets, bandages, stretcher, a single page from the armory record her father had kept in the late forties.

Untitled, 1999, digital print, 24x13

The Day After

Uncle Malachi was the first to arrive
Jumping from his bike that kept running.
Wearing dark sunglasses and
With a quivering voice he said: That's it.

Uncle Eitan came from the kibbutz
In borrowed pants, too large for his size.
Crumpled and terribly funny
They flapped in the wind.
He made it in the nick of time.

Uncle Yigael tried but couldn't.
Sodom was too far and cut off.
One Piper plane had already crashed.

This year I made a pilgrimage to the grave
Together with my three uncles,
And loved them to tears.

(ca. 1971)

The Shelter – A Poem with Four Alternative Endings

It's the strongest, he said,
And the safest too.
My father planned a cylindrical shelter.

He made in the ground a big hole,
Cast a round floor with
A pillar of concrete in the middle.

He built around it a wall
With a narrow staircase
And a safety exit.

Ending #1
And on Sabbath eve, in the month of Tammuz,
When he went and did not return,
We tried to cast the ceiling by ourselves.

Ending #2
And on Sabbath eve, in the month of Tammuz,
He was called on duty
And left the shelter roofless.

Ending #3
And on Sabbath eve, in the month of Tammuz,
He picked up his rifle
And, like God, we finished the job on the Sabbath.

Ending #4
And on Sabbath eve, in the month of Tammuz,
He gathered all of us in the shelter,
And himself ascended through the open roof
Never to come back.

(ca. 1971)

Jerusalem, Bezalel, 1955-1959

No-Man's Land, Jerusalem, 1956, photograph, 25x15

1955 was as yet a year of relative innocence in the annals of a seven-year-old State of Israel, where Socialism and national patriotism still retained central roles: that year, the Histadrut labor federation inaugurated its Executive offices in Tel Aviv, and the Lachish settlement area in the northern Negev was launched for the purpose of absorbing immigrants from North Africa. The Tel Aviv art scene was still in uproar over the abstract revolution of the "New Horizons" group, which was also seven years old. The city of Haifa played no more than a minor role in that revolution, through local artist Zvi Mairovich.

When sixteen year old Ziva Shisha left Haifa for Jerusalem, to study at "New Bezalel," that institution was celebrating its twentieth anniversary (in the annals of the academy this constituted a second chapter, whose achievements could be credited mainly to Jewish immigrants from Germany). A new floor was added to the institute, which was to be directed over the next two years by calligraphy teacher Yerachmiel Schechter. Over two hundred students were registered that year at "New Bezalel," whose departments comprised applied graphics, metallurgy, and weaving (the ceramics department was launched in 1958). Ziva Shisha registered with the graphics department, under the direction of Rudi Deutsch-Dayan, where painting was taught by Shlomo Vitkin and Michael Gross, while Isidor (Yitzhak) Ascheim and Yossi Stern taught drawing and illustration. Yehuda Bakon would start work as drawing teacher in 1959. In 1956, Yaakov Pines joined up as an additional instructor in woodcuts, alongside the veteran Jacob Steinhardt. During the years 1957-58, a number of students from the graphics department agitated for the establishment of an art department, but that would not come about before 1967. Accordingly, in 1958, Bezalel's acting director Rachel Kedem expelled the student Zvi Tolkovsky for the offence of refusing to attend graphic design classes.

Entering "New Bezalel" before even graduating from high school, Ziva Shisha realized her childhood dream of studying applied art. Ever since she was ten, she had been attracted to the magic of transforming an idea into a succinct visual graphic image. Her studies and upkeep in Jerusalem were facilitated by a Defence Ministry loan for orphans of fallen Israeli soldiers. She was among the youngest of her class in the graphic department – which included Danny Kerman, Avner Katz, Mordechai Moreh, Moshe Hoffman, and Noga Adler. "We were afire, we couldn't wait any longer," she would recall years later, referring to herself, Danny Kerman and Avner Katz, with whom she kept up a close friendship over many years.

Painting classes in the applied graphics department focused on graphic techniques of printmaking (lithographs, woodcuts) and drawing. Kronzon devoted four years to her studies, producing a series of works that displayed considerable talent. A black-and-white print of a self-portrait (1959) exhibits lyricism and melancholy, verging upon an elegiac sense of self-expression: the artist's head emerges from a black background (the dark stain seems to flow downwards), her regard, downcast in gloomy contemplation, seems to reveal her biographical burden, enfolding the entirety of her future course. Certainly, the mood of the self-portrait transcends the spirit of lighthearted mischief that Yossi Stern instilled in the department's drawing students, with the blessing of the instructors of poster design, including Rudi (Reuven) Deutsch and Friedel Stern. Other woodcuts created by Ziva Shisha during her studies at Bezalel are faithful to the language of her mentor Yaakov Pines (himself a student of Jacob Steinhardt), featuring Jerusalem's urban vistas of alleyways and houses

The Herman Struck Prize, 1959

that cast their shadows by day and by night. The alliance between lyricism and shadow seems to transcend the familiar Bezalelite mannerism of the time: it reveals shadows in the artist's psyche, their traces also evident in the woodcuts she created to illustrate a poem from Nathan Alterman's poem "The Joy of the Poor," as an exercise for the calligraphy class under Yerachmiel Schechter: the "stranger" – The Dead (death being the "joy of the poor") – embraces his beloved as a black, mysterious figure, the pair waving to one another; the young artist remains true to the duality of life and death, here and there.

An additional woodcut illustrating that poem, in identical format, focuses on the "stranger jealous of the grace of his spouse." The "stranger," a monumental spirit, is The Dead – brandishing a menacing arm. Pencil drawings from 1956-59 mostly represent self-modeling in various postures, somewhat theatrical (possibly recalling the deportment in sketches by Egon Schiele). These works, charged with qualities characteristic of works by her drawing instructor Isidor Ascheim, are proof of superb sketching ability, and yet fail to expose a ponderous inner world – which finds its expression in her woodcuts, less direct but more dramatic in their black-and-white contrasts.

Bezalel student Ziva Shisha was noted for her gifts. By 1958, she had won the academy's prize (acquisition of her work) and a year later she was awarded the Struck prize – the most prestigious award Bezalel offered its students. She received it for an oil on canvas depicting looms from Bezalel's weaving department. The structures – with the figure of a weaver in the background – compose a constructivist arrangement resembling scaffolding for a building (or the remnants of a building?); an amalgam of the "feminine" machine and the notion of construction (home). In its flattened, angular and stylized figurativeness one can identify something of the influence of her painting instructor, Shlomo Vitkin.

When Ziva Shisha, a mere twenty, concluded her studies at "New Bezalel" in 1959, she found herself on the hoped-for path of graphics. That year, Yosef Zaritsky won the Israel Prize for painting. The "New Horizons" group was at the pinnacle of its influence, and lyrical abstract was the dominant language of the Israeli avant-garde. Ziva Shisha, having studied figurative, even illustrative art, was entirely out of touch with the avant-garde. At the time, she saw her vocation in the domain of graphic design.

Self Portrait, 1959, lithograph, 40x24

Self Portrait, 1958, graphite, 49x32

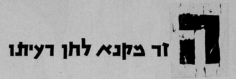
זר בקנא לתן רעיתו

אל תלבשי את שמלת החג.
אל תצחקי לעולם.
מסביבך יחנף ויפתה וילהג,
ואני בעגל עולבים לך חג.
ואני על קוו כבו עיט חג,
במלמך מבני חם ונוצרך מקהלם
לבל תראי שמש, לבל תדעי חג,
לבל תצחקי לעולם.

אם תנוסי אל סתר בית,
אם במבת רעים תשבי,
לא תנוסי מקול העיט,
הבצעק לך: אשתי, אשתי!

"Dead's Envy" (Alterman), 1959, woodcut, 50x30

"Dead's Envy" (Alterman), 1959, woodcut, 50x30

...ניתך ברד אבנים על זגוגיות החלונות.

Illustration for Esther Streit-Wurzel's **Boys of the Underground**, M. Mizrahi Publishing, Tel Aviv, 1971

Tel Aviv, Illustrations, 1960-1971

Immediately upon concluding her studies at Bezalel, Ziva Shisha was inducted into the Israeli army as graphic designer at the Defence Ministry's Ma'arachot Publishing House, which resided in an old stone house in the Kiryah military compound in Tel Aviv. At Ma'arachot Publishing she got to know writer and editor Adir Cohen, who opened up her path into the publishing world. She started illustrating the volumes of stories and legends that Cohen gathered and edited, published initially by Shimoni Publishing and subsequently by M. Mizrachi Publishing, both located in Tel Aviv. After a year and a half of military service, she applied for special leave to illustrate Adir Cohen's *Flowers on the Path of Slavery*, published by Eked Publishing. When the army turned down her request, "I got married and got myself discharged." However, two weeks later, the graphic artist – now Ziva Kronzon, though she continued to sign her work Ziva Shisha (or just Ziva) – returned to her job at Ma'arachot Publishing, now as a civilian employed by the army on a full salary.

After her discharge from the army, she worked as graphic designer at the celebrated Tel Aviv publicity agency Shaham-Levinson-Ayalon; also employed there was another designer, Riki Ben-Ari,[9] who exercised an influence on Kronzon, attracting her towards graceful decorative illustration. In the early sixties, as we shall describe in detail, Kronzon illustrated children's films, and in the late sixties she also did illustrations for *Sami and Susu*, a popular children's television show. In 1970-71, along with all her other jobs, Kronzon now illustrated books for Masada Publishing House. It was thus a period of grueling labor, day and night, as the young illustrator rushed from office to office, from one task to the next. And all that before even mentioning uncompromising motherhood of two toddlers – Iris (born in 1965) and Rafi (born in 1967).

All this time she resided in Tel Aviv – "a city I'd fallen in love with even when I was living in that old house in the Kiryah, while my husband, who was studying medicine at the Hebrew University, lived in Jerusalem. He studied and worked, and I worked at anything I could find in my field. In one instance, I corrected an entire edition of a book where there was a spelling error, using

9   Ricky Ben Ari, (1936-2005), graduate of fashion studies at the Beaux Arts in Paris, made her name in early sixties Israel with her illustrations for newspapers and children's books. From 1965 onwards, Ben Ari concentrated on fashion design.

10 See footnote 1.

a nib pen."[10]

Here follows a partial list of the books (most of them for children and young people) for which Ziva Shisha-Kronzon drew illustrative drawings and colored covers in the 1960s:

- Adir Cohen, *Flowers on the Path of Slavery (Negro Legends)*, Eked Publishing, Tel Aviv, 1960.
- Adir Cohen, *A Selection of Russian Legends*, M. Mizrahi Publishing, Tel Aviv, 1961.
- Adir Cohen, *A Treasure of Legends for Children*, M. Mizrahi Publishing, Tel Aviv, 1962.
- Adir Cohen, *A Selection of Oriental Legends*, M. Mizrahi Publishing, Tel Aviv, 1963.
- Adir Cohen, *A Selection of North American Legends*, M. Mizrahi Publishing, Tel Aviv, 1963.
- Adir Cohen, *A Selection of Italian Legends*, M. Mizrahi Publishing, Tel Aviv, 1964.
- Yitzhak Levanon, *Basket of Spells*, M. Mizrahi Publishing, Tel Aviv, 1964.
- Yitzhak Levanon, *Polichinelle at the King's Court*, M. Mizrahi Publishing, Tel Aviv, 1965.
- Adir Cohen, *Funny Stories*, M. Mizrahi Publishing, Tel Aviv, 1965.
- Avner Karmeli, *The Daring Foursome*, M. Mizrahi Publishing, Tel Aviv, 1966.
- Yitzhak Levanon, *The Khalif of Baghdad*, M. Mizrahi Publishing, Tel Aviv, 1967.
- Nathaniel Hawthorne, *The Golden Fleece*, M. Mizrahi Publishing, Tel Aviv, 1967.
- Yitzhak Levanon, *Birbal the Wise*, M. Mizrahi Publishing, Tel Aviv, 1969.
- Yemima Avidar-Tchernovitz, *Operation 52*, Masada Publishing, Tel Aviv, 1970.
- Alexander Dumas, *The Three Musketeers*, Masada Publishing, Tel Aviv, 1971.
- Uriel Ofek, *A Letter in the Land of Wonders*, Masada Publishing, Tel Aviv, 1971.

In her book illustrations, she focused on the narrative, on a particular line she had picked out from the text, adopting, with deft figurative talent, a "cheerful" line (some of these illustrations were caricatures, such as those she made for *A Letter in the Land of Wonders*, into which she integrated letters and words), a "youthful" contour with distant echoes of the drawings of Yossi Stern (a swift, affably expressive line, elongated figures) and even more distant echoes from the illustrations of Nahum Gutman. These illustrations left the designer no scope for self-expression: they featured a graceful, friendly, undulating penciled outline, and images replete with activity and ornamentation – crowded with figures, animals, houses and landscapes. Shadows are almost non-existent and the dynamic lined representation emphasizes the vivid anecdote. The specific situation, abounding in multi-dimensional action, is more important than delving into the psyche of some character or other. Overall, the inclination towards complex scenes means very little focus on individual portraits. Faithful to the framework of tales derived from every corner of the world and diverse epochs, Ziva Shisha-Kronzon opted for elementary historical representation (a Greek hero, a Venetian gondolier from Renaissance times, etc.), tending towards the exotic (remote European towns and villages, figures and mosques from Baghdad, an African mother). A more realistic approach was adopted in designing the cover of *Boys of the Underground* by Esther Streit-Wurzel (Masada Publishing, 1970), depicting a ritual underground swearing of allegiance by the light of an oil lamp. Here, Ziva Shisha-Kronzon's 1948 War experience drew out more profoundly dramatic qualities, certainly less jovial, particularly on the cover (but also in the illustrations throughout the book – notably the drawing of Arabs attacking a bus standing in the heart of an Arab village – which are of a higher quality than most of her "exotic" illustrations). Likewise, her designs for Yemima Avidar-Tchernovitz's *Operation 52* exhibit fine qualities, as in the illustration *We Call for Peace*, depicting a political demonstration. In these books, Kronzon was nearer to herself, in a cultural environment and time close to her heart, close to the burning embers of memories, which for the moment are mostly suppressed.

Throughout the sixties, Kronzon never halted her outpour of illustrations, both drawings and watercolors. In 1965 she started creating, for the Israel Filmstrips company, a series of visuals for stories from the Book of Genesis,

42   Cover for Charles Deulin's **The Little Soldier**, M. Mizrahi Publishing, Tel Aviv, 1966

Cover for Nathaniel Hawthorne's **The Golden Fleece**, M. Mizrahi Publishing, Tel Aviv, 1967

שִׁבְעָה חִצִּים מָרְעָלִים הָיוּ תְּקוּעִים בְּגַבּוֹ

46   Illustration for **A Selection of Chinese Legends**, edited by Adir Cohen, M. Mizrahi Publishing, Tel Aviv, 1968

"יושב אני וְחְמָס."

Illustration for **Funny Stories**, edited by Adir Cohen, M. Mizrahi Publishing, Tel Aviv, 1965

From illustrations to **The Family** magazine, New York, 1975-2000

Illustration to **The Stampfer Family History in Petach Tikva**, private publishing, 2000

From illustrations to **The Family** magazine, New York, 1975-2000

Illustrations for Uriel Ofek's **A Letter in the Land of Wonders**, Masada Publishing, Tel Aviv, 1971, 24x18

Illustrations for Uriel Ofek's **A Letter in the Land of Wonders**, Masada Publishing, Tel Aviv, 1971, 24x18

Genesis (The Story of Noah), filmstrip, 1965-70, courtesy Michael Tal, Israel Filmstrips

Genesis (The Story of Noah), filmstrip, 1965-70, courtesy Michael Tal, Israel Filmstrips

Genesis (The Creation of the World), filmstrip, 1965-70 (reconstructed color), courtesy Michael Tal, Israel Filmstrips

Genesis (The Creation of the World), filmstrip, 1965-70 (top: reconstructed color), courtesy Michael Tal, Israel Filmstrips

Untitled, 1962, ink, 50x35

Drawings for Stories by Kafka, Agnon, and Others

Untitled ("The Trial"), 1962, ink, 50x35

Untitled , 1962, ink, 50x35

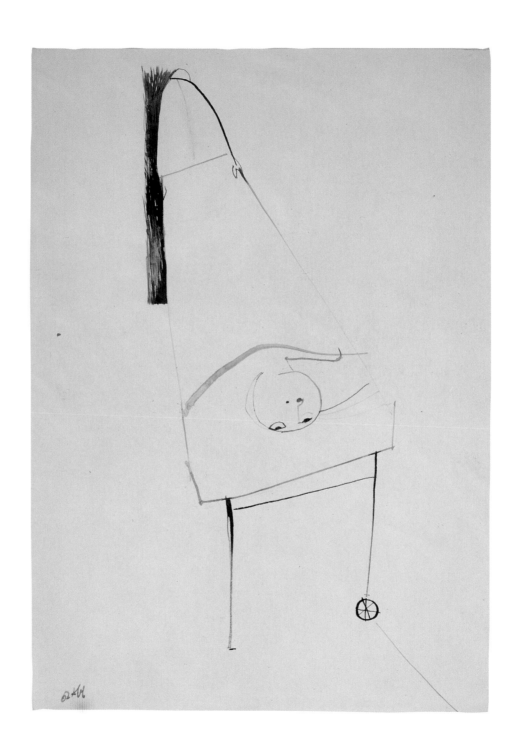

Untitled ("Tehila"), 1962, ink, 50x35

Untitled, 1962, ink, 35x50

Untitled, 1962, ink, 50x35

Untitled, 1962, ink, 50x35

Untitled ("Tehila"), 1962, ink, 50x35

Untitled (Kafka), 1962, ink, 50x35

Untitled ("Only Yesterday," Stray Dog), 1962, ink, 35x50

Untitled ("Only Yesterday," Stray Dog) 1962, ink, 35x50

Untitled ("Only Yesterday," Stray Dog), 1962, ink, 35x50

Untitled ("Only Yesterday," Stray Dog), 1962, ink, 35x50

Untitled ("Only Yesterday," Stray Dog), 1962, ink, 50x35

A.P.   Ambivalence   Zvi Kanar

Ambivalence, 1973, aquatint, 41x35

New York, Etchings, 1973-1978

At the end of 1971, shortly after Kronzon had completed her caricaturistic illustrations for *A Letter in the Land of Wonders*, the Kronzons relocated to New York with their two young children, aged six and four. Their original intention was to return to Israel as soon as Dr. Itzhak Kronzon completed his period of fellowship at the department of cardiology of New York's Einstein Hospital in the Bronx. For the time being, the couple resided on the 12th floor of the staff building on the hospital grounds, and Kronzon, despairing of finding work in graphics or animation (in spite of attending a summer course in animation at the School of Visual Arts), resolved to study the technique of etching. She consulted two Israeli artists of her acquaintance from her time at Bezalel, now print instructors at the academy – Zvi Tolkovsky and Aryeh Kilemnik, who had returned to Israel from lengthy sojourns in the United States. They told her of the Brazilian master printer Roberto Delamonica, who now taught etching at the Art Students League of New York.

Seven whole years, day by day, five days a week, Kronzon applied herself at the school workshop in the heart of Manhattan; an open workshop, focusing on imparting etching technique. However, her growing mastery of the medium brought with it forms and content that combined to launch a significant artistic chapter, offering a springboard for Ziva Kronzon's career from here on.

Unconnected with developments in New York's galleries, which owing to the pressures of her existence lay beyond Kronzon's reach, her etchings affirm Surrealism. Its roots may be sought in the a-realistic and poetic qualities she had expressed as far back as 1962 in her illustrations to the works of Agnon and Kafka (writers themselves touched with Surrealism), as well as her illustrations dating from that early period to H.N. Bialik's "The Legend of Three and Four" (including, for example, a representation of the skeleton of an ox in the shape of a ship). In other words, the transition from applied art to fine art did not come about as a sharp change or as starting from scratch; rather, it was a further elaboration of materials that had already sprouted in Kronzon's work and developed over the course of her seven years' work at the Art Students League workshop, and subsequently in her private studio.

exposing figures packed within it. All the limbs of the body supporting the brain from below are duplicated.

A number of shared characteristics stand out from this review of the forms and content of the etchings:

A. Surrealism resorting to exotic illumination that glows out of nocturnal darkness. A sense of revelation, magic and dream. Subsequently, in 2002, Ziva Kronzon would put on an exhibition of photographs titled "Night Vision"; in these etchings, she already seems to "see in the dark." The colorfully lustrous exoticism was inspired by a trip to India she took with her spouse in 1973 (the choice of India was indebted to their shared love of Rudyard Kipling's *Kim* and their acquaintance with an Indian friend in New York). Likewise, many of the compositions – division and a multitude of limbs, mystic eyes, flowers and other exotic plants, the erotic etc. – are indebted to Indian mythological images.

B. Kronzon's artistic language is still partially rooted in illustration, even if stemming from personal sensation. From this viewpoint, the etchings were an interim stage in the artist's development towards expression that is self-aware both formally and materially.

C. Kronzon's transition from the two-dimensional etching to the three-dimensional embossed print displays an attraction to materiality, which will intensify in the course of her career.

D. The motif of Eros, pregnancy and birth is conspicuous throughout the series. The frequency of the motif is indebted primarily to the symbolical, even mythical, centrality of the subject in world cultures (Indian visual culture included). But even more so, the motif of pregnancy and birth responds to the dread of annihilation and destruction that Kronzon has had since childhood. "Pregnancy is simply the counter-response to death," she would say many years later. That does not, of course, contradict the fact of the artist's own pregnancy in 1975, the year she bore her youngest child, her daughter Shira. Be that as it may, "feminine" expression grows out of Kronzon's work right from the outset, proclaiming the force of creation, the force of life.

E. In these etchings, the subject of pregnancy and birth is incorporated in

Mourning, 1972, aquatint, embossed paper, 13x30   73

motifs of mourning and death. Alongside the work entitled *Mourning*, populated with masks of grief, the etchings are replete with vistas of mystery and dread. The dividing, melting bodies are also a form of organic decay, and the nocturnality is also a subconscious shadow of death. Admittedly, this morbidity is not the dominant content of the etchings, but its evident presence suggests a force that was to grow more externalized in Ziva Kronzon's work.

Elegy, 1974, aquatint, rolled ink, 23x23

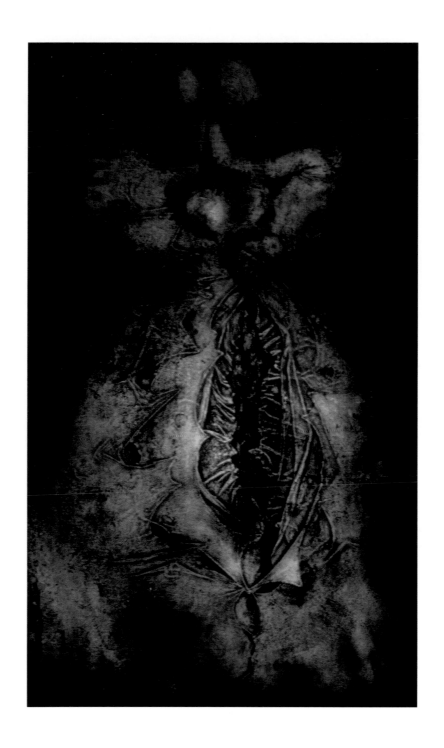

Torso, 1975, collagraph, aquatint, 51x30

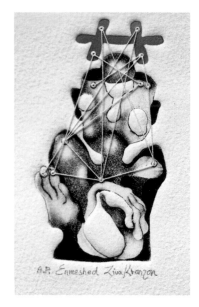

Miniature etchings, 1975, approx. 8x4 each. Top, left to right: **Enmeshed**, **Embroiled**, **Torso**;
Bottom, left to right: **Uncle Arthur Reconstructed**, **Anathema**, **Icon**

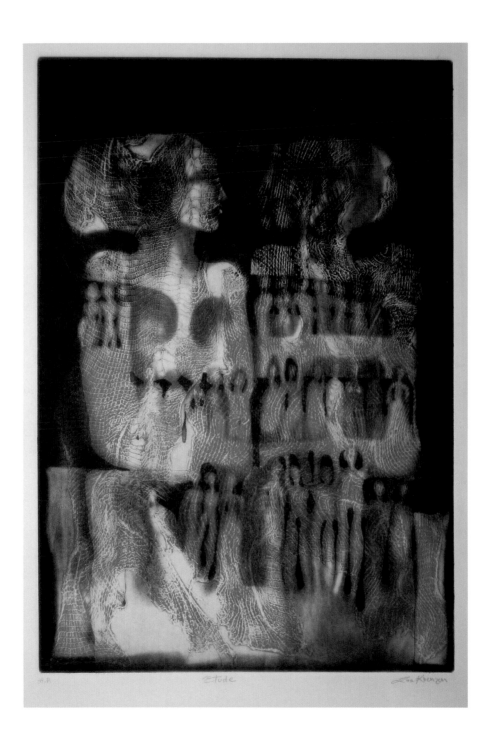

Etude, 1973, collagraph, aquatint, 45x30

Nocturne, 1974, aquatint, embossed paper, rolled ink, 31x13

Stage, 1972, aquatint, embossed paper, rolled ink, 63x37

Untitled, 1977, aquatint, 45x30

Etchings: Sheets and Containers

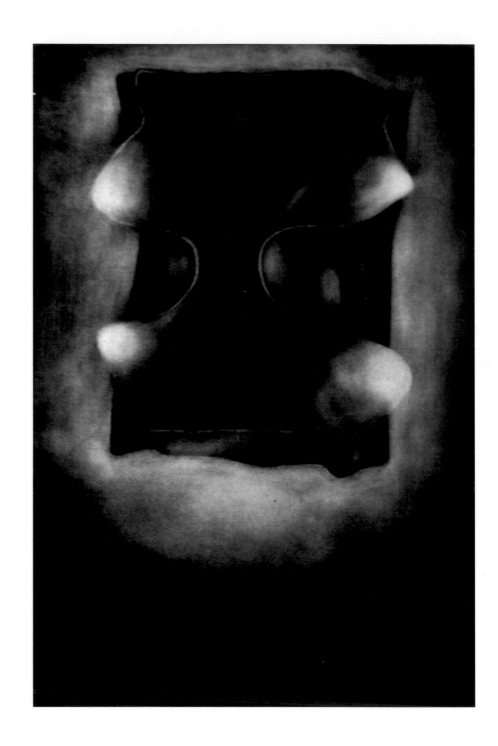

Untitled, 1977, aquatint, 45x30

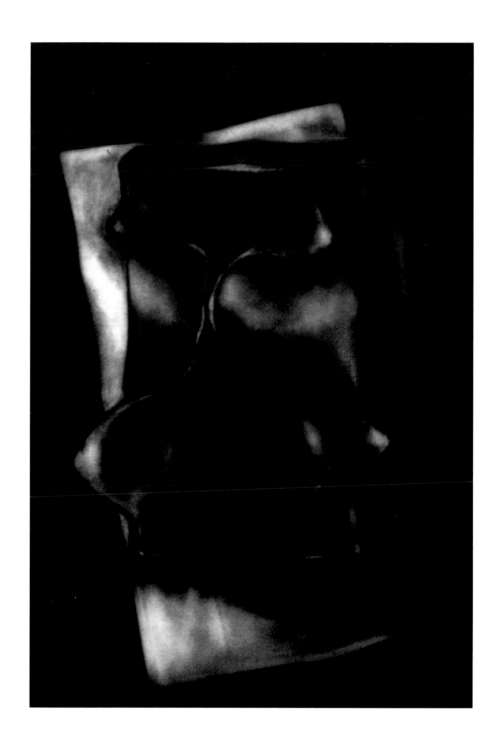

Untitled, 1977, aquatint, 45x30

Monoprint   Brown Paper   [signature]
                                                            NY. 1978

Brown Paper, 1978, monoprint, 45x30

Towards "Blind Drawings," 1978-1981

1978 heralded a progressive turn in Ziva Kronzon's creative work. She was still engaged at the Art Students League workshop, but something began to change in her surrealist etchings: increasingly, the organic, tender images were harnessed to more geometrical forms and structures. In New York, post-minimalist art had reached maturity, grid structures had become bon ton and geometrical compositions were now a familiar language. Consciously or not, Kronzon's prints took on a rather more contemporary presence.

Box and vessel motifs, which had already appeared in the etchings of the seventies, were stressed in those of 1978. In an untitled aquatint, a "rusty" box hovers, radiating shimmering light out of the surrounding darkness. The box is wrapped in "cloth," whose edges open up to reveal the emptiness within the box. In their form, the cloth edges are still linked to the surrealism of earlier etchings, as are the mystical hovering and lighting. However, Kronzon's lexicon of images has begun to take shape in a new, decisive direction.

To an increasing degree, the sheet image began to dominate the 1978 aquatints. Against a black background, four long, narrow strips shimmered as they fell like four minimalist ribbons that had undergone a "feminine" conversion to greater smoothness, featuring in some dramatic scene recalling an illuminated curtain. A further possibility (relying on the reversed location of the artist's signature): the four strips sprout upwards like four soft verticals. Either way, the cloth, the envelope, is the "skin" left over from the X-rays of the female body of previous etchings.

In print after print, the cloth image is reiterated as a kind of an organic envelope – layer upon layer – enclosing a guarded secret, while hovering in a black expanse. It is clear to the viewer that Ziva Kronzon was fascinated with the tension of revelation and concealment, as she forged her way towards minimalism. The fiery "Indian" colors make way for monochrome, principally black-and-white. At the same time, the image becomes simple and abstract, and the content seems to affirm an interest in art on art: a two-dimensional surface (the cloth image) upon another two-dimensional surface (the print paper). However, this is an interim stage, where dualism is still characterized

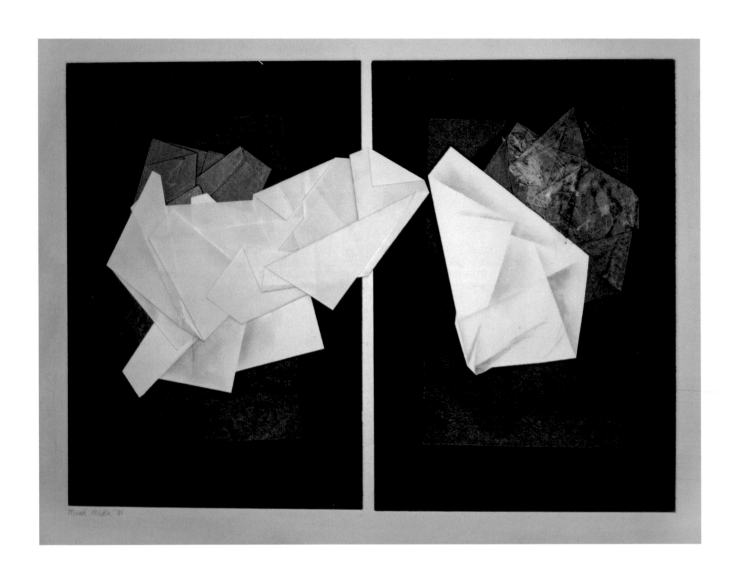

94   **Diptych**, 1978, monoprint, folded paper, pencil, 45x60

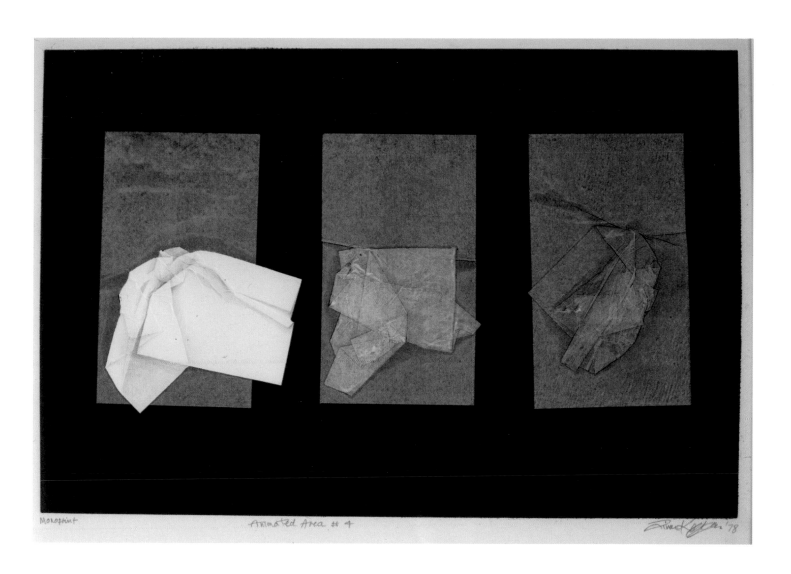

Monoprint   Animated Area # 4

Animated Area #4, 1978, monoprint, pencil, embossed paper, 30x45   95

Monoprint

Untitled, 1980, monoprint, 30x45

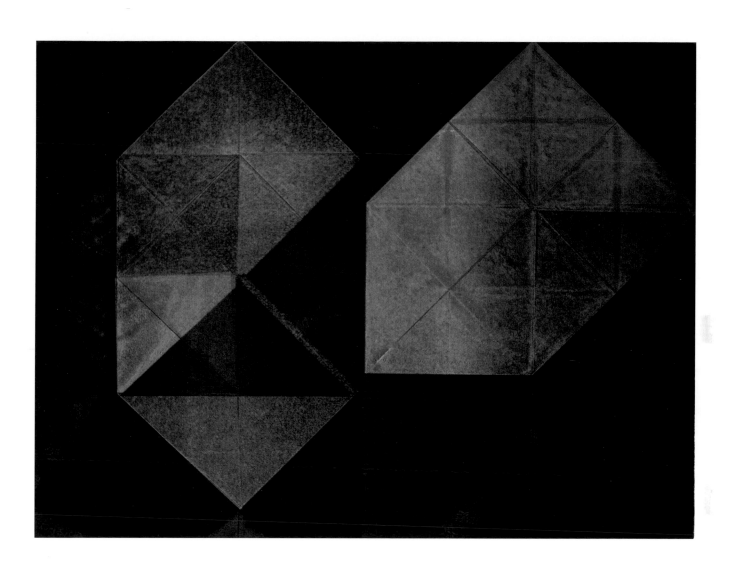

Folding #1, diptych, 1978, monoprint, 45x60

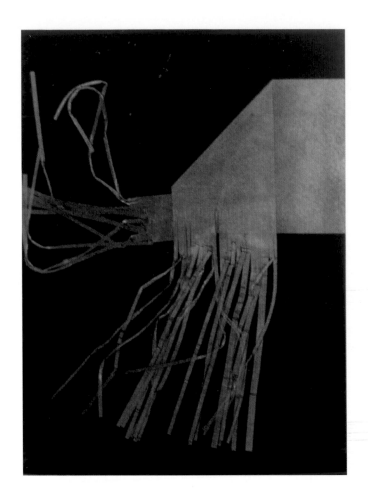

Diptych, 1978, monoprint, 45x61

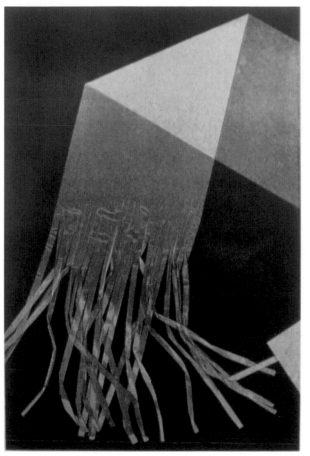

Diptych, 1978, monoprint, 45x61

Deviation #1, 1978, monoprint, 45x30

Deviation #4, 1978, monoprint, 45x30

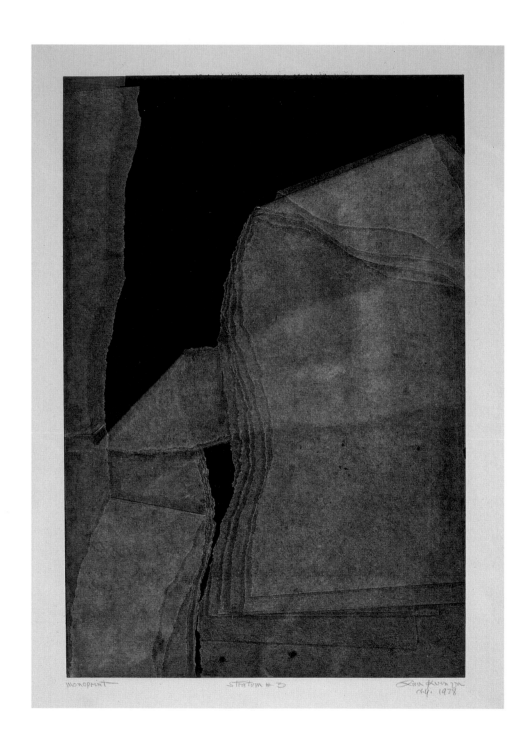

monoprint   Stratum #3   [signature]
calif. 1978

           Stratum #3, 1978, monoprint, 45x30

Stratum #2, 1978, monoprint, 45x30

Untitled, 1978, monoprint, 45x30

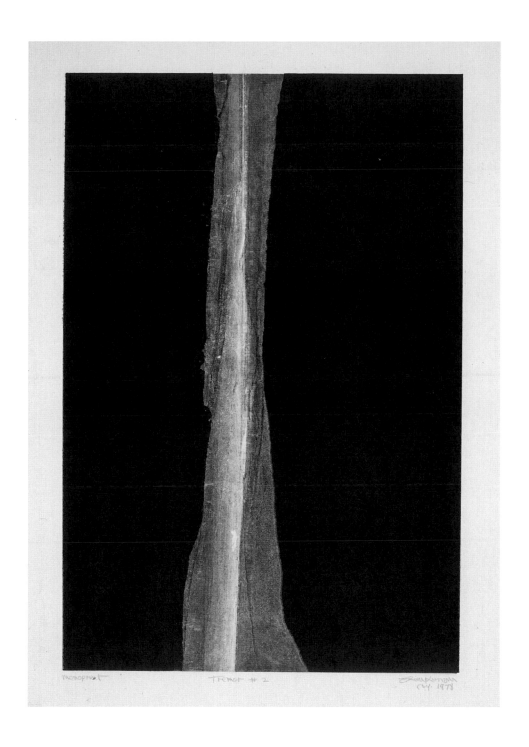

Tremor #2, 1978, monoprint, 45x30

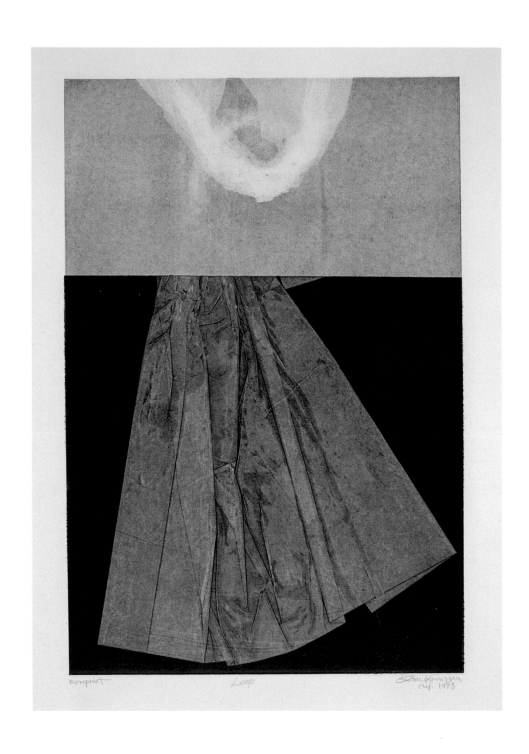

Reflection on White, 1978, monoprint, 45x30

Gray Loop, 1978, monoprint, 45x30

Animated Area, from the series "Blind Drawings," 1979, embossed paper, collage, 45x30

Untitled, from the series "Blind Drawings," 1979, embossed paper, chine-collé, 45x30   109

Untitled, from the series "Blind Drawings," 1979, embossed paper, collage, 45x30

Untitled, from the series "Blind Drawings," 1979, embossed paper, pencil, collage, 45x30

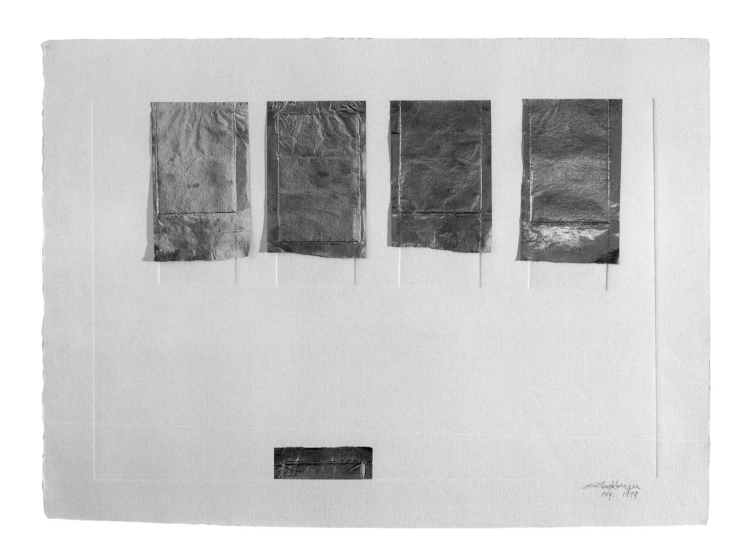

Untitled, from the series "Blind Drawings," 1979, embossed paper, copper leaf, 30x45

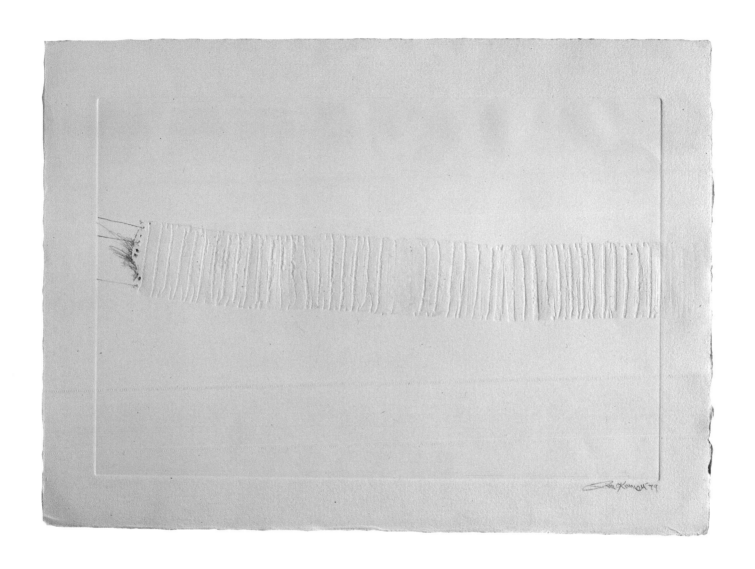

Untitled, from the series "Blind Drawings," 1979, embossed paper, pencil, 30x45

113

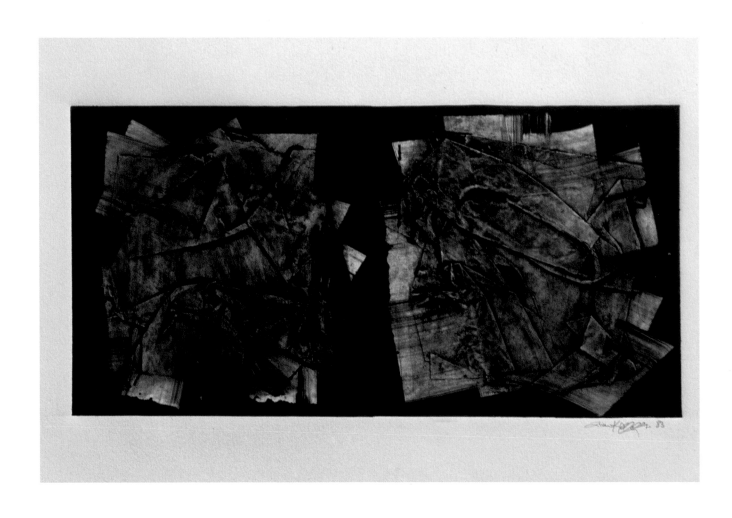

114   **Untitled**, 1983, collagraph, rolled ink, 23x46

Untitled, 1983, collagraph, chine-collé, rolled ink, 23x46

Madonna without Child, 1985, monoprint, collage, rolled ink, 23x35x0.5

A.P.   *Animated Area*

Animated Area, 1983, collagraph, collage, rolled ink, 23x23x1   117

118 **From the Inner Vault**, from "Incas' Chronicles," 1982, embossed paper, copper leaf, threads, ink, 30x40

"Incas' Chronicles," 1981-1983

Following her period of preoccupation with white paper prints, Kronzon began to integrate into her work threads of cotton (the very same cotton that serves as raw material for the manufacture of paper), the thread replacing the line of the earlier etchings and even serving a pseudo-semiotic function. This creative chapter gave rise to the "Incas' Chronicles" series, displayed in May 1982 at Vorpal Soho gallery in New York, and then at the Julie M. gallery in Tel Aviv. The series comprises collages based on hand-made paper and colored threads. The collages were produced in several stages: preparation of the paper pulp, casting it in molds, and finally processing it and integrating glued, woven and sown threads into it: "The artist confronts paper, the medium of the written word, with the spun thread, a primitive form of symbolical representation."[18]

18 From the leaflet to Kronzon's exhibition at Vorpal Soho, New York.

Kronzon's reference to Inca culture arose from knowledge retained from her youth, and her impressions of the 16th century Central American empire whose culture was unfamiliar with the written word. As a lingual substitute, the Incas resorted to *quipu* – cotton spun threads to which multiply knotted colored strands were attached, used principally for quantitive measure. The quipu served mainly for count of inventory items and census counts. The Kamayoqs, Inca officials charged with deciphering the quipu, taught their descendents how to decipher it, leaving behind no written records of Inca life. "The Inca had no writing," Kronzon told an interviewer years later, "but I created an archive of pseudo-history. They were a small people who took control of their surroundings, subjugated other tribes and laid new roads into their territories. I dealt with the Incas' excessive expansion, which led to their downfall."[19] Was Kronzon referring to a Mideastern context, all too familiar to visitors to her Tel Aviv exhibition? "The work is *very* political," she stressed many years later, also referring to the paradoxical contrast between a culture that had no written language (or paper) and works on paper with (written) titles. The notion of fictional interpretation was to seize Kronzon's attention in the future.

19 See footnote 1.

In June 1982, Kronzon exhibited the show "Incas' Chronicles" at Julie M. gallery in Tel Aviv. The combination of threads and handmade paper, featuring in various textures and hues, were perceived as the artist's personal "words."[20]

20 Rachel Azuz, review in *Davar*, 14 June 1982 [Hebrew].

21 Rachel Engel, review in *Ma'ariv*, June 1982 [Hebrew], undated clipping from the artist's archive [Hebrew].

22 Undated clipping from the artist's archive.

The exhibition drew enthusiastic reviews. "The most delicate exhibition we have seen in many years," wrote Rachel Engel in *Ma'ariv*,[21] while Gil Goldfine of *The Jerusalem Post* commented: "Ziva Kronzon's 'Incas' Chronicles' are the most delicately and sensitively constructed works of art seen at a local gallery in a long time."[22] The sheets of paper (30x45 cm) recurred throughout the series in varying thickness, sometimes with frayed, unfinished edges. The threads (even flax, in one of the works) were generally integrated in minimalist serialism, with knots at their extremities and often resembling dried plants. Chequered and grid structures were also pressed into the paper, joining an overall duality of order and chaos. In a work entitled *The Fraud*, four rows, with threads embedded into three of them, were pressed; another work, *Drought*, was composed of dark paper, a crumbling rope at its head and some thirty threads dangling from its base; *Restoration Account* comprised fibers changing progressively from dark on top to light below; in *Index* a thick red thread was woven, which seemed to draw a line of hills on the paper. Rachel Engel described the general appearance of the works:

> Very thin threads dangling from the roof of the picture, over the length of the paper. The knots in the threads are the entire modulation, with ochre stains and incisions in the paper (small suggested squares).[23]

23 See footnote 20.

In some instances, Kronzon continued to press crumpled paper or torn and frayed gauze onto handmade paper, both embossed and impressed (in addition to the adhesion of threads). In others, she integrated the handmade paper, as yet unrefined, in the structure of a rectangular imprint impressed into a foundation of refined, finished paper. The variations were numerous, including the tearing of the handmade paper and separation of its parts (with the threads as bridging lines) over the aforementioned impression. And although she occasionally resorted to brown hues, throughout most of the series she preserved the purity of white-on-white, an abstract minimalist formula familiar ever since Kazimir Malevitch's Suprematism, a favourite with the artists of Bertha Urdang gallery in New York (the domain of numerous Israeli artists of the "Beyond Drawing" school), where Kronzon exhibited her work in the years 1988-91.

The archive concept underlying the series served Kronzon as the notion

The archive concept underlying the series served Kronzon as the notion of systematic cataloguing and classifying, whereby the threads (and the less prevalent ropes) were arranged in some order or other (in the work entitlted *Damaged Archive* the threads were swallowed up in total chaos within the paper before it had been completely refined). Almost without exception, the "Incas' Chronicles" series avoids ethnographical representation of Inca culture. Kronzon resorted to this culture principally as a pretext for minimalist and material creativity, with an ancient primitive tribality echoed within its modernist appearance (Structuralism, peaking in western art of the eighties, seems to have offered Kronzon broad scope for her artistic undertaking). Standing slightly apart was a work entitled *Flight of the Kamayoqs*, which comprised in an abstract manner three fleeing figures (i.e. three folded papers with limb-like threads extending from them, above and below). In another work, *Absence of the Kamayoqs*, many red threads encircle an empty center, like sun rays surrounding a circle. *War Effort*, another work from the series, featured a dark red patch, amorphous and dramatic, over a reddish rectangle printed on paper, with a mass of threads dangling from its base. The war motif, we recall, will be revealed in time as the supreme subject of Ziva Kronzon's work.

Two days after the opening of the exhibition at the Julie M. gallery, the 1982 Lebanon War broke out. In consequence, Kronzon went through a period of artistic paralysis of sorts, spending the year in numerous experimental ventures – a prolonged process of path seeking.

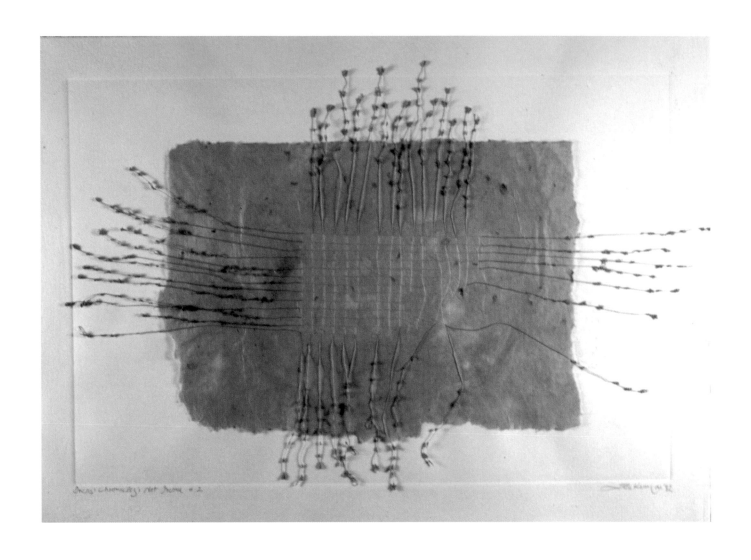

122   **Net Income #2**, from "Incas' Chronicles," 1982, embossed paper, threads, 30x40

Incas' chronicles: Joint Income

Joint Income, from "Incas' Chronicles," 1982, embossed paper, threads, 30x40

124 **Conflicting Reports**, from "Incas' Chronicles," 1982, embossed paper, threads, 30x40

Fertile Field, from "Incas' Chronicles," 1982, paper, threads, cotton, 30x40

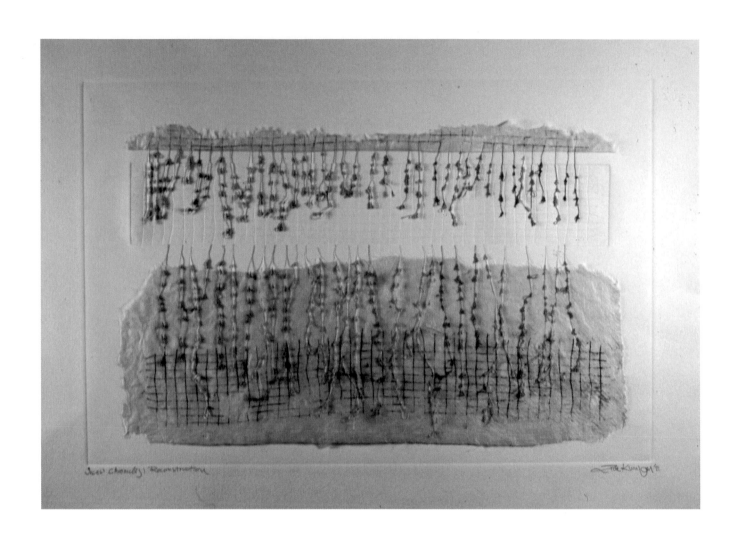

Good Crop Reconstruction, from "Incas' Chronicles," 1982, embossed paper, threads, 30x40

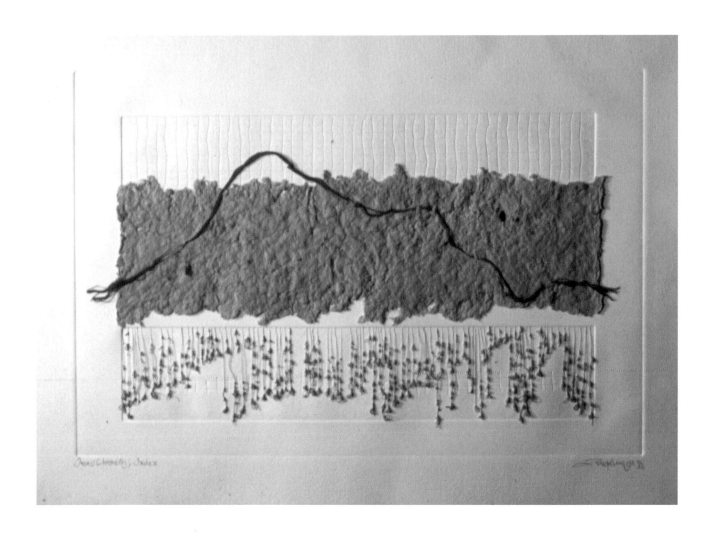

Index, from "Incas' Chronicles," 1983, embossed paper, threads, 30x40

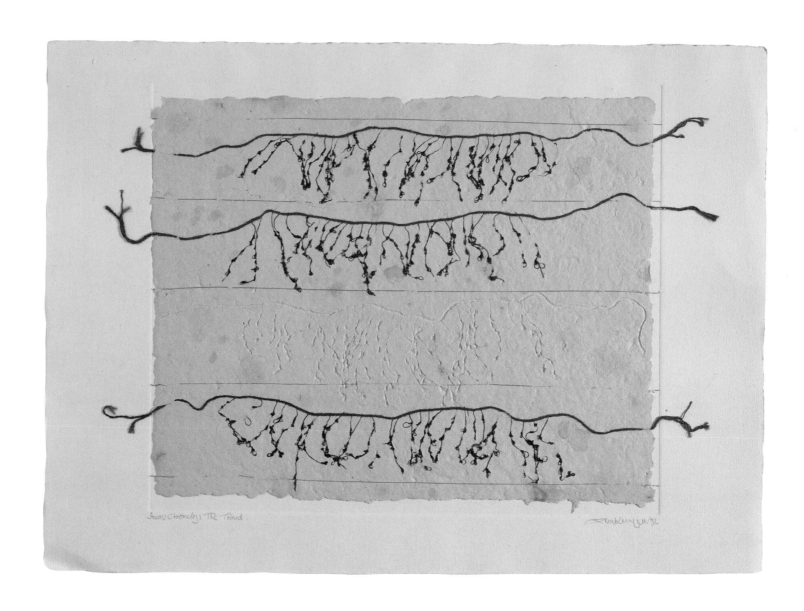

The Fraud, from "Incas' Chronicles," 1982, embossed paper, threads, 30x40

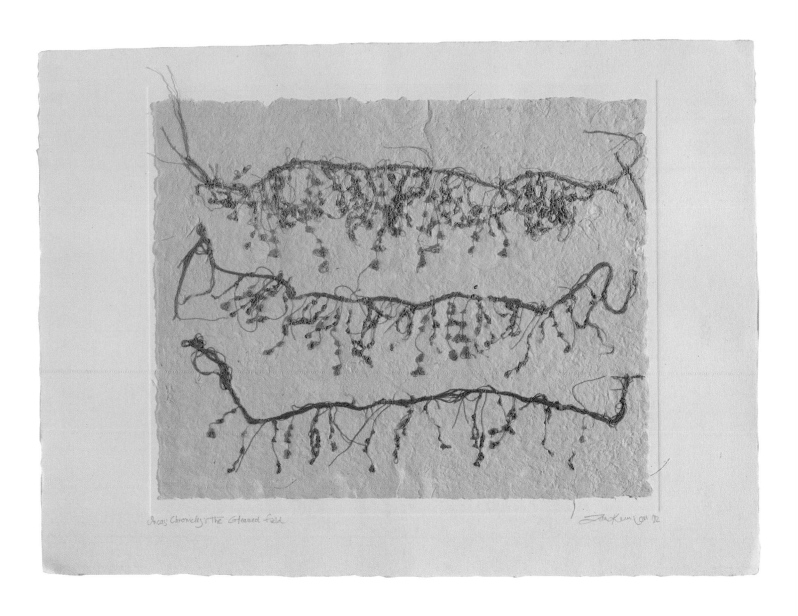

Incas Chronicles The Gleaned field

The Gleaned Field, from "Incas' Chronicles," 1982, embossed paper, threads, 30x40

129

The Prized Bride, from "Incas' Chronicles," 1982, embossed paper, pencil, threads, printing paint, ink, 30x40

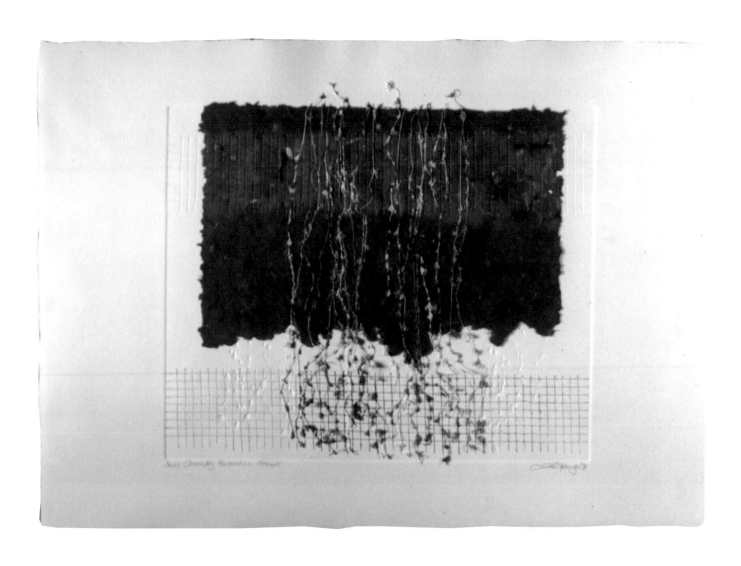

Restoration Account, from "Incas' Chronicles," 1982, embossed paper, printing paint, threads, 30x40

134   **First Year of Famine**, from "Incas' Chronicles," 1982, embossed paper, threads, fibers, 30x40

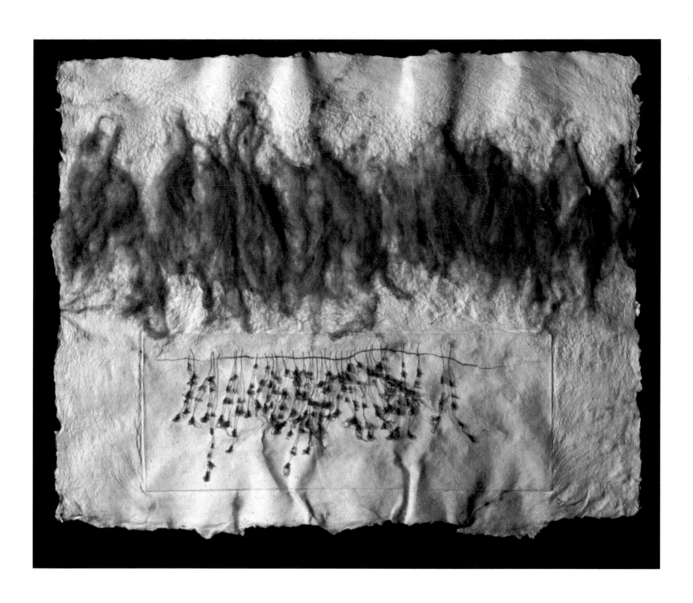

Disintegration, from "Incas' Chronicles," 1983, paper, threads, fibers, 35x40

Dry Season, from "Incas' Chronicles," 1984, paper, cotton, lacquer, threads, 35x40

Distorted Balance Sheet, from "Incas' Chronicles," 1982, embossed paper, threads, 30x40　　　　　　　137

Kamayoq's Flight, from "Incas' Chronicles," 1982, embossed paper, threads, 30x40

Damaged Archive, from "Incas' Chronicles," 1982, embossed paper, threads, 30x40

140

From Collagraphs to Containers, 1983-1985

"Floating Spaces," National Art Center gallery, New York, 1980

Was it the 1982 Lebanon War that inspired in Kronzon such distress that she was led to create and display objects associated with disaster and calamity? Kronzon recalls:

In the Lebanon War, the whole of Israel underwent a national process that can be likened to the experience of anyone who has suffered personal loss. I sensed that my personal story had fused together with that of others. This fusion between personal and national feelings paralyzed me over the course of a year. I wasn't up to creating anything. I worked in paper and trashed it, working and trashing, until one day I found myself constructing vessels resembling the boxes used by Christians to safeguard holy relics. The message emerging was clear: if the material designated to preserve the sacred is paper, what kind of preservation is that? And so I began constructing monuments out of paper....All my life I've been haunted by two women: the image of the mother of Sisra, looking out of her window and expecting her son, who is late in arriving; and the mother who lost ten sons in the collection of epic poems from Kossovo (translated into Hebrew by Shaul Tschernichovsky). A question has been hammering at me all my life, to which I've never received a convincing answer: where was Sarah when Isaac was offered up as sacrifice?[24]

24   Ziva Kronzon in an interview with Rivka Raz, "Where was Sarah when Isaac was Offered Up?" *Yedioth Ahronoth*, *Zmanim Modernim* supplement, 3 May 1989 [Hebrew].

Kronzon's progress to the "paper monuments" went by way of collagraphs and chin-collé (a combination of print and collage) where silk papers, folded and crumpled, in shades of gray, rust brown, metallic and black, were printed and pressed. Most of these collagraphs emanated an air of destruction or residues of disaster impregnated with soot and blood. Over and over again, these works reiterated symmetrical, though not identical, pairings of layers of paper, folded or crumpled, with or without black brush strokes. In the 1985 collagraph *Madonna without Child* the crumpled, printed silk paper seems to represent the image of a woman, most of it outlining a piece of clothing – or, to be precise, the sleeves of a blouse. The emphasis on this detail paved the way for subsequent works by Kronzon, which would show actual blouses and sleeves. For the time being, the heightened material character and the overall

<   **Bandage**, 2000, digital print, 36x24

141

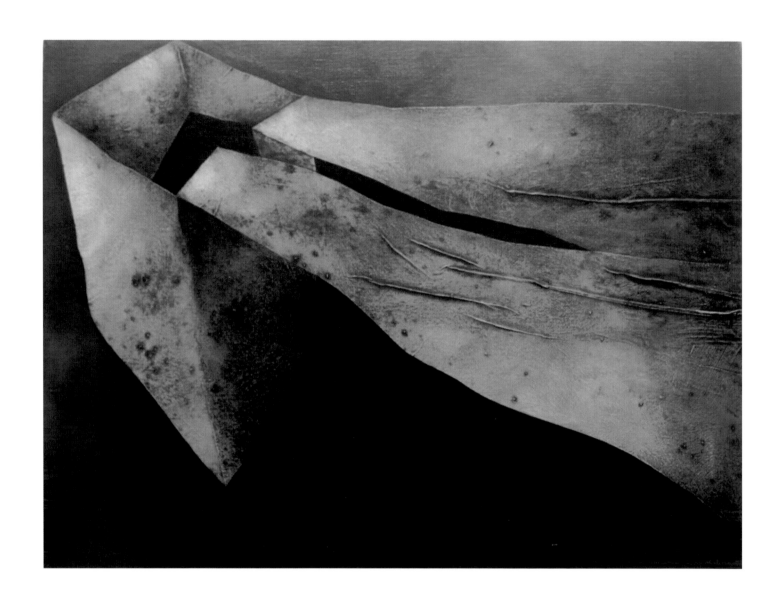

Untitled, 1980-81, oil and collage on canvas, 46x60

and chaos, fibrosity and mass, enormity and smallness. It should be noted that adopting the concept of the absurd would also characterize Kronzon's own interpretation of her work, as will be elaborated below.

Apart from resorting to soft, vulnerable materials (in response to a "masculine" art world), Eva Hesse adopted a serial minimalist – though "warm" – language: in her 1969 *Expanded Expansion* Hesse created a kind of partition or corral-like fence structure composed of rubberized cloth inserted between fibreglass columns. Thereby, the artist integrated minimalist serialism with materiality and primitivism. The work expands and contracts like an accordion from one installation to the next. In *Contingent*, another work dating from the same year, eight strips of latex-covered cloth hang past each other, their upper and lower portions made of fiberglass.

Above all, a comparison should be drawn between Kronzon's cast paper vessels and those created by Eva Hesse: *Repetition 19 I* (1967) consists of 19 vessels, most of them somewhat squashed, made of papier-mâché and polyester on aluminum netting. *Repetition 19 III*, another work similar in spirit from 1968, comprises similar vessels fashioned of polyester. We should also recall an untitled work from 1968 consisting of three vessels made of latex, with ropes emerging and connecting them one to another. In *Metronomic Irregularity* (1968) two rectangular vessels are connected together by masses of threads. And in *Sans II* (1968) rectangular vessels of fiberglass and polyester hang close together from a wall.

It is important to specify that Kronzon "discovered" Eva Hesse years after having herself become deeply immersed in the vessels motif. As we recall, the box and vessel motif had already sprouted in her seventies etchings. Only at a later stage of her etching studies at the Art Student League, in the late seventies, she was amazed to encounter the work of Eva Hesse (through Lucy Lippard's book on the artist's work), and "from that moment on, I began to observe the close affinity between my works and hers."

There can be no doubt about the close family kinship between the postminimalist (or "minimalist-expressive," as Donald Kuspit preferred to describe them) vessels of Kronzon and those of Eva Hesse. And yet, there are significant differences: in the paper's simulation of metal in Kronzon's work; in the catastrophic motif therein; in its traumatic autobiographical origin.

Untitled, 1985, cast paper, pigments, 25x70x45

Archive Fever

"Incas' Chronicles" launched Kronzon's major archival project. For from now on, for twenty years and more, she would incessantly arrange and catalogue the large "storehouse" of her "finds." From exhibition to exhibition, she would build up her "museum" – or rather, "mausoleum" – archive of a past catastrophe and a catastrophe to come. As we shall see in the next chapters, Kronzon's archive is open to the public. She is simultaneously archeologist, archivist and curator. The three etymological aspects of the term "archive" – *arkhē*, *archon*, and *arche* – come into effect in Kronzon's archival project: at the arkhē level, Kronzon's archive is dominated by her passionate desire to return to a primal past, ancient origins, a "black hole" where, possibly, the artist will meet again with her father and re-experience the moment of parting from him; her archive is ruled by her, for she is the *archon* (ruler) who constructs the archive – but even more so by the arch-*archon*, her absent father, whose departure and death in the war opened up a long, openended chain of memory, at its core the daughter's memory but not hers alone, like a space where one travels in time in order to find the fundamental truth of the specter of her dead father; here is the archive's existence as *arche* – a coffin, turning the entire archival enterprise into an act of mourning.

However, the works of archival mourning far transcend the spectral patri-archivism of a yearning to meet a dead father, who dominates the archive and whose spirit is evoked by whoever accesses the archive. Because, at the very heart of archival activity, death lurks – or at least destruction and absence, as Jacques Derrida demonstrated in his book *Archive Fever*.[30] For the imperative of memory and preservation is just one aspect of the dynamic bi-polarity of the archive; at the other pole are the forces of repression, censorship and concealment – and above all, imposition of the return and concealment of the source in impenetrable and inaccessible darkness.

The archive, simultaneously open and sealed, constitutes an object of nostalgia, but also of countless contradictory interpretations that enforce a waiving of any return to an original. Accordingly, every archive is in a state of tension between a constituting past and an unknown future (of revelation of the

30 Jacques Derrida, *Archive Fever: A Freudian Impression*, translated by Eric Prenowitz, University of Chicago Press, Chicago & London, 1996.

sole and absolute truth of the father of the archive), which is the "messianic" dimension of archival action. The spirit of the dead father, as the source of archival authority, awaits the countless "sons" and "daughters" who will come to interpret – in their different and contradictory ways – the well-kept secret: the truth buried in the archive. The compulsion to return – that fatally paralyzing obsession – will repeatedly push the son-daughter back to the archive, to that multi-layered mound of repression and concealment, dismantling and erasure, at whose roots lies the great darkness: "…the archive is made possible by the death, aggression, and destruction drive…anarchiving destruction belongs to the process of archivization and produces the very thing it reduces, on occasion to ashes, and beyond."[31]

That is the violence of the archive, its open wound, its chronic malaise: archeological and messianic yearnings side by side, controlled simultaneously by nostalgia and violence. The task of cracking the secret of the archive (which is doomed to failure) employs various kinds of theatrical rhetoric means, but these are condemned from the outset to the paradoxical *aporia* of memory and its burial (repression).

Are not the previous lines a description of Ziva Kronzon's artistic endeavors? Could we not also apply to her efforts the destructive compulsion to return, the obsessive yearning to return to the place of commencement – the disastrous constitutive scene of the loss of father/archon?

> The *trouble de l'archive* stems from a *mal d'archive*…. It is to burn with a passion. It is never to rest, interminably, from searching for the archive right where it slips away. It is to run after the archive…It is to have a compulsive, repetitive, and nostalgic desire for the archive, an irrepressible desire to return to the origin, a homesickness, a nostalgia for the return to the most archaic place of absolute commencement.[32]

In her "archival" endeavors, is Kronzon not motivated by the dualism of the pleasure principle (creativity, painting, image, camouflage, simulation) and the death drive (destruction, aggression, violence, disintegration, ruin)? Does not each of Kronzon's exhibitions constitute an invitation to a space of preservation and revitalization of specters, in the course of which no encounter will take place other than an immersion in the signs of destruction and dissolution?

31 *Ibid.*, p. 94.

32 *Ibid.*, p. 91.

Thus, the compulsive archival return will not result in the artist's recuperation; rather, it will heighten her yearning and paralysis. And each new exhibition will be a psychic self-portrait – but one which is ever more fragmented, more battered, more defeated.

Reliquary Cover, 1985, cast paper, pigments, 25x25x10

Angel, 1985-2004, cast paper, pigments, 25x35x13

Puta Doll, 1985, cast paper, pigments, 72x18x16

Reliquary #2, 1985, cast paper, pigments, 72x65x27

Torso, 1984, cast paper, pigments, threads, nacre, 60x25x25   157

Reliquary #3, 1985, cast paper, pigments, 50x80x24

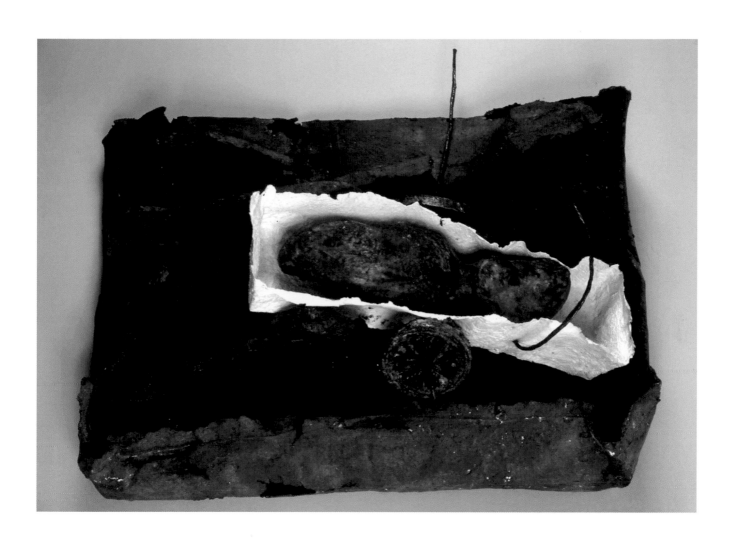

Untitled, 1985, cast paper, pigments, 20x78x36

Baskets, 1985, cast paper, pigments, 88x48x25

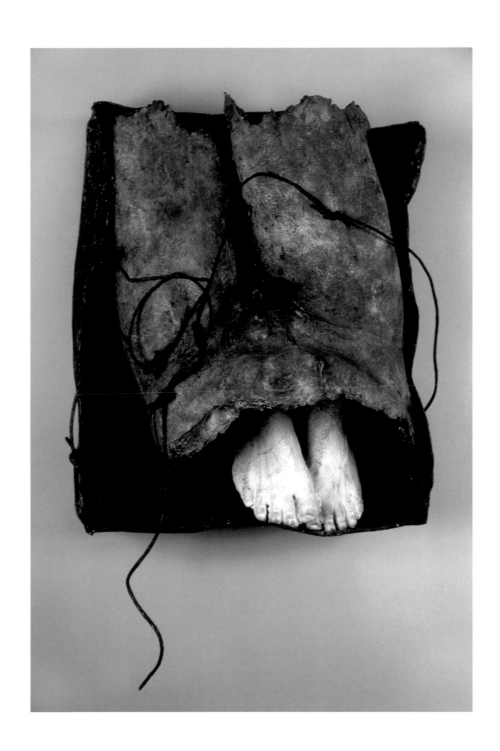

Reliquary, 1984, cast paper, pigments, 50x43x23

Untitled, 1985, cast paper, pigments, threads, 40x40x26

Reliquary, 1985, cast paper, pigments, 26x37x37

Reliquary with Wheels, 1985, cast paper, pigments, 45x25x25

Two Cases, 1988, cast paper, pigments, bronze, 20x35x25

Empty Pods, 1986, cast paper, pigments, 28x70x70

Untitled, 1988, cast paper, pigments, iron wire mesh, 20x20x15

Ruptured Space, 1988, cast paper, pigments, 80x80x70

Loss, 1986, lead, cast paper, pigments, 75x100x75

Fragments, 1989, Hydrocal plaster, pigments, 35x140x70

Matrices, 1989, Hydrocal plaster, lead, pigments, 25x25x33

Seat, 1988, wood, cast paper, iron, 70x95x38

Untitled, 1987, cast paper, pigments, cardboard, 200x40x36

184   Ziva Kronzon installing the exhibition "Close Formation," Bertha Urdang gallery, New York, 1992

Between Hades and Hephaestus, 1990-1991

In the late eighties, Kronzon had a series of exhibitions affirming a new central chapter in her work. In 1988 she exhibited at the Bertha Urdang gallery in New York, where she would display her "vessels" again in 1990, the same year she would exhibit at the Nora gallery in Jerusalem. Commenting on the first exhibition, at Bertha Urdang, which comprised iron-like paper vessels combined with structures of plaster and lead, *New York Times* critic Michael Brenson described the process of casting the paper vessels in plaster molds, comparing their surface to scorched, scarred flesh; the exhibition as a whole he regarded as a kind of "war-zone playpen."[33] Brenson referred to Kronzon's affinity with Eva Hesse, John Chamberlain (metal sculptures from remnants of crashed cars) and John Duff (abstract sculptures of fiberglass and other materials, some hanging on walls), noting some of her works, such as *Pile*, which reminded him of dynamite sticks. In a review in *Ma'ariv*, Shlomit Shaked commented on the same New York exhibition, focusing on *Vessels* (1986) – twenty black paper buckets thrust into one another like links, along the wall's entire height. Associations of blood and war enveloped the exhibition, the sense of grief being reinforced by titles like *Removal*, *Loss*, etc. Use of military webbing in structures (*Totem*: a horizontal modular composition of webbing-like parts) guaranteed the warlike context. One of the works was even entitled *Katyusha*.

All these aspects found concise expression in Kronzon's 1990 exhibition at the Nora gallery in Jerusalem. Outstanding here was a central structure entitled *Hatch*, a structure cast in paper and blackened to create a burned/ metallic effect, as desribed in detail by Miriam Yizrael, critic for the local weekly *Kol Ha'Ir*:

> A grayish-black wall structure, scarred and sagging, obscuring the window and darkening the gallery space. It was constructed especially for this purpose. What prevents the observer from drawing away from the structure, which conveys deterrence, is a small hatch cut into the wall, attracting the viewer's gaze with its promise of a possible egress into different space and light....As the observer

33 Michael Brenson, *The New York Times*, 28 October 1988.

Close Formation, 1990-91, cast paper, pigments, 70x300x550

Block, 1989-90, polyester resin, pigments, 25x100x100

Circle, 1987, cast paper, pigments, iron wire, 25x120x110

Bucket, from "Dispersion," 1993, cast paper, pigments, 27x25x27

Buckets (detail), 1994-95, floor installation, polyester resin, pigments, iron, 40x235x95

Decoy House, 1990-91, polyester resin, pigments, 71x46x102

Shelter, 1989, Hydrocal plaster, lead, pigments, 72x50x50

Shell, 1989, cast paper, pigments, 60x48x40

Untitled, 1989, Hydrocal plaster, pigments, 50x80x55

Portable Monument, 1989, Hydrocal plaster, pigments, 77x50x32

Reliquary, 1986, cast paper, pigments, 45x25x25

Hatch, 1989, cast paper, pigments, 300x250x20

Aligned Bodies, 1988, cast paper, pigments, 25x48x275

Gemini, ca. 1982, cast paper, pigments, 50x36x20

Pouch, 1993, cast paper, pigments, wax, 30x30x13

210   **Flat Pouch**, 1993, cast paper, pigments, wax, 60x35x1

Two Pouches, 1992, cast paper, pigments, 35x60

212   **Untitled**, 1993, mixed media, 40x40

Untitled, 1993, mixed media, 40x52

Yellow Pouch, 1993, mixed media, 60x35

Untitled, 1990, cast paper, pigments, 100x70

216   **Untitled**, 1990, cast paper, pigments, 35x50

Habitat, 1990, cast paper, pigments, 25x75

Shooting Post #1, 1990, cast paper, pigments, 60x60x3

Shooting Post #2, 1990, cast paper, pigments, 60x60x3

Shelter #1, 1990, cast paper, pigments, 60x40x3

Shelter #2, 1990, cast paper, pigments, 60x75x3

Blue Container, ca. 1991, cast paper, pigments, 33x33x25

Blue Container, 1991, cast paper, pigments, 41x41x15

Untitled, 1987, cast paper, pigments, 80x65x40

Untitled, 1990, cast paper, pigments, 92x42x22

Empty Pod, 1991, cast paper, pigments, 127x127x25

Small Crater, Large Crater, 1989, rubber, 25x120x70

Matrix, 1990, cast paper, pigments, 157x51x25

Appendage, 1988, cast paper, pigments, 200x33x50

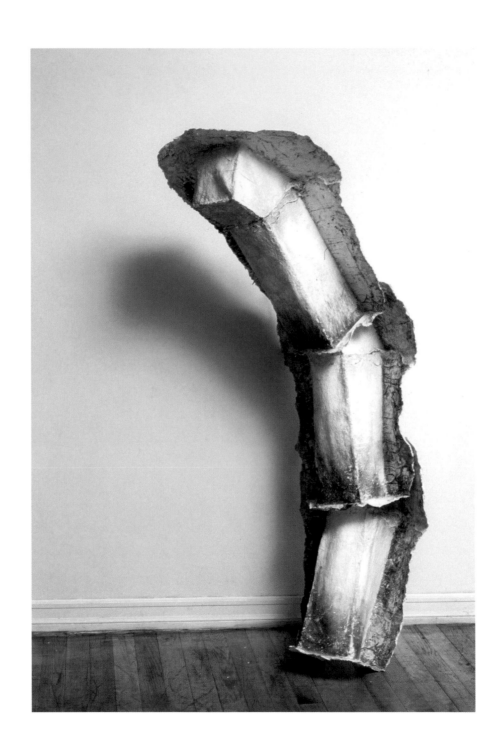

Dislocated Body, 1990-91, cast paper, pigments, 178x66x76

Milestone, 1989, Hydrocal plaster, pigments, 50x28x28

Vessels, 1986, cast paper, pigments, iron, 200x40x220

Arch, 1989, polyester resin, pigments, 15x26x200

Burrow (After Kafka), 1990-91, cast paper, pigments, 50x300x360

Projection, 1988, cast paper, pigments, 194x38x96

244   **Personal Shelters** (detail), 1997, cast paper, pigments, iron, dimensions variable

The Burden of Time, The Burden of Space

The footprints of Kronzonian time are destruction, injury, dissolution and death. The rust hue, featuring in the metallic appearance of the cast paper containers, is just one aspect of a complex process of corrosion (whose concrete manifestation as actual rust is apparent, for example, in the 1991 sculpture *Reinforced Structure*, comprising a cubic envelope of cast paper enveloping an iron web like skin. The web's rust is noticeable on the white paper.) The containers are battered, torn, split, broken, wounded, perforated, crumpled etc. (*Line Formation* from 1990 displays four Hydrocal plaster units flattened to resemble a house – all broken and cracked). Time, entropic in essence, strikes objects and man alike.

The archeological aspect of Kronzonian works affirms three kinds of time: a) past time, of the home that was; b) interim time; c) time of the remnant displayed. The first assumes an optimistic, vital coming-into-being, affirming life; someone built a house, someone had resided in the house, until the fire came, until the destruction. That is, past time bears an illusion of stability and creation, but sooner or later the illusion will be shattered and the house demolished. Interim time is the time of interment, an a-historical time during which the ruins await exposure. However, this non-time too has been eroded by entropic time, in the form of rust and corrosive blemishes. It is the time of the decaying corpse. And the time of display is the time of the "archeologist" (delving into her past), who displays to us both her finds and the instruments (containers) of her excavation (which are transformed into burial containers?). The latter – baskets of sand – take us by surprise, whether because they too look like battered remains, no less damaged than the finds they are designated to expose, or because they are arranged in a neat grouping, empty of all rubble or find, seemingly abandoned by the absent archeologist.

So when was this "dig" conducted? Why are the baskets empty? And what lies behind their neat, aesthetic immobility? The answer to the first question appears to be that excavation into the past also bears tidings of the future, which is the identical message of festering and bitter end. Accordingly, the "burned" baskets displayed before our eyes are a kind of archeology of the wall. This is a pod that originally grew on a tree, and it is thus obvious that its lying on the ground represents a pre-burial phase. We should also point out that "pod" not only denotes a seed housing, but is also the term for the housing from which combat planes drop their bombs...

Flying Buttress, 1987, was a vertical structure bending into an arc to lean against a nearby wall; the structure comprises nine "tin" containers on top of one another, with a crooked iron strand emerging from each container. The modular vertical structure extends upwards, like some "botanical" architecture (the strands as branches), recalling a Brancusi's *Colonne sans fin*. However, the column/trunk folds lightly into the adjoining wall, and is thus also doomed to a reversal of support roles.

The insubstantial cast paper is also related to the emptiness of the "tin" containers – that is, the emptiness of the column. These characteristics are reinforced by the act of emptying out signified by the tins which, while designed for storage, fail to fulfill their function. The abortive erection is thus accompanied by impotence (the vacuity of the fertilizing force, like the vacuity of the previous "pod"). Other failed erections may be found in works such as *Vessels*, 1986 (19 paper castings of buckets, forming a pipe that crawls from floor to wall and upwards), *Leaning Duct*, 1988 (eight rounded vessels constituting a "pipe") and *Projection*, 1988 (23 round containers sprouting upwards towards the adjacent wall, like a pipe cut off at its highest extremity). These are phallic pipes, just as *Burrow (After Kafka)* dating from 1990-91 (two modular pipes comprising numerous "links," crossing one another on the floor like a pair of gigantic worms) is a conveyor of liquids (water? blood? sperm?) decomposing into their components. (In his story "The Burrow," Kafka creates a paradoxical situation in which a subterranean creature burrows itself in a set of tunnels in order to defend itself against an enemy; overpowered by anxiety, it also prepares many emergency exits, only to become afflicted with a new anxiety: that its enemy might invade its domain through these very exits.) In this context, we should stress the human dimension suggested by the slumped, crumpling stance of the "columns." Their varying heights – 187, 157, 132, 203 cm etc. – maintain a consistent affinity with human height. Certainly, a structure like *Dislocated Body* (1991, height 178 cm) indicates this affinity in its very title, as well as by its structure of three "limbs" ending at the upper

Reinforced Structure, 1991, cast paper, iron, 61x91x76

Incubus, 1994-95, cast paper, wood, steel, 195x157x75

Slain upon her High Places

The postmodern eighties brought with them a new concept of sculpture, seeking to respond to the material "authenticity" of the seventies (rusty iron, concrete etc.) – not to mention the classicist notion of the sculptural grappling with matter – with fictitious materiality, which took on the character of "sculpture as theatrical scenery." On that point, I wrote the following in 1983:

> It takes no more than a superficial glance at the new sculpture coming into being in recent years, to understand that materials like tin, cardboard, fur, plywood and even soft pinewood set aside the notion of heroic grappling with the material....Above all, it is hard to dismiss the feeling that contemporary sculpture is often similar to theatrical scenery....Thus, the anti-Platonic dimension arises within present-day sculpture: the dimension of holding on to the image, to the illusory and fleeting, in response to an idyllic clinging to the world of fixed, eternal Platonic Ideas.[40]

40 Gideon Ofrat, "Sculpture as Theatrical Scenery," in *Reflections*, Israeli Art, Jerusalem, 1982, pp. 41–43 [Hebrew].

This was the period when Kronzon's art was maturing towards sculpture in cast paper, fabricated to look like a functional object in rusty metal. It was theatrical sculpture, resembling scenery, which affirmed this observation. Like scenery, it fitted into the language of objects that had become the "protagonists" of Kronzonian drama:

> Unlike sculptures aspiring to the human body, scenery avoids representation of man. As such, it is a rare aspect of theatrical performance – representing not man, but objects. However, all that is purely superficial. For scenery is the non-human revealed to us as human:...in the course of the performance, material scenery objects undergo a transformation and become a human idea.[41]

41 Gideon Ofrat, "Between Environmental Art and Theatrical Scenery," in *The Artistic Medium*, Stavit, Tel Aviv, 1987, p. 130 [Hebrew].

Something underlying the postmodern message refused to attribute to sculptural fiction (and all artistic fictions, of any kind) representation of substance, regarding the masquerading envelope as an expression of lingual breakdown, which condemns every language, including the languages of art, to a "play of signifiers" which are forever divorced from their signifieds and whose shared

Personal Shelters, 1997, cast paper, pigments, iron, dimensions variable

Cluster (detail), 1995,
mixed media

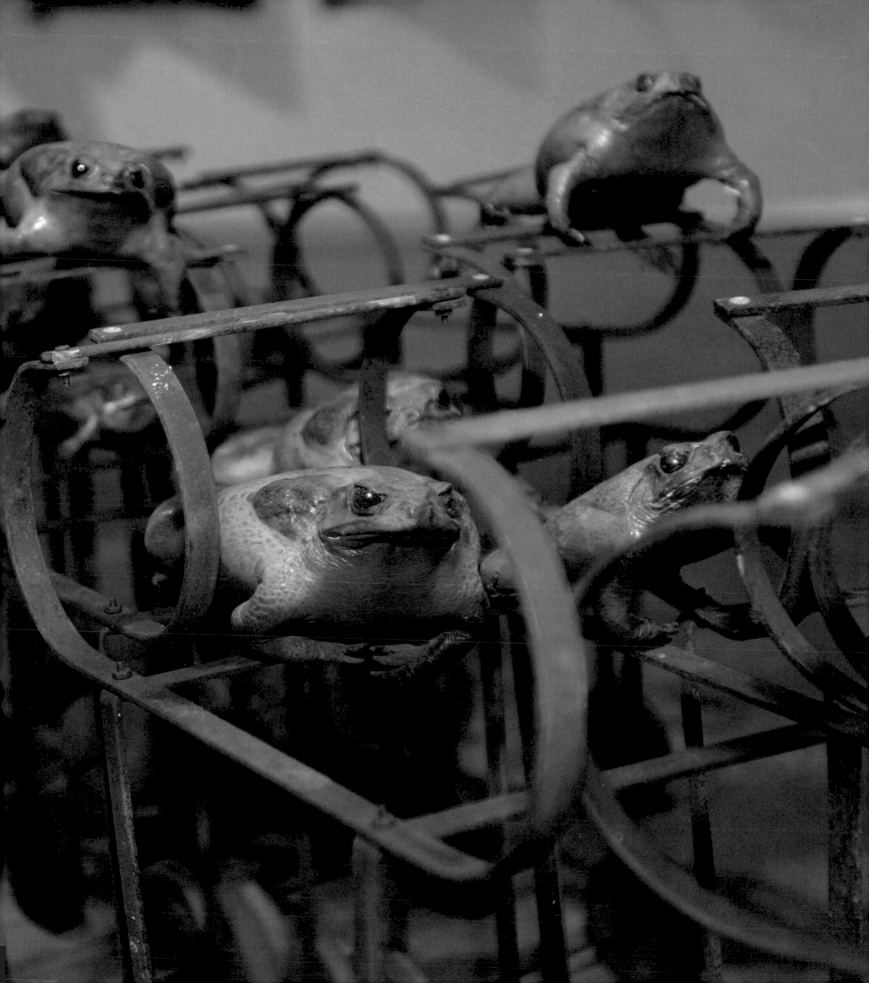

Cluster, 1995, mixed media, dimensions variable

Skeletons, 1994-95, mixed media, dimensions variable

Military Pouches, 1998, digital print, 65x100

Art and War

Images of war have never lost their hold on Western art since its very beginning, including its antique roots in the art of Egypt and Mesopotamia, in paintings and bas-reliefs depicting the triumphs and the heroism of god-kings (like the Assyrian ones from Nimrud, from the ninth century B.C.). Remarkable examples of this tradition are the representations of war in Greece of the fourth and fifth century B.C., such as the stone reliefs with their tempestuous mythological battle scenes from the frieze of the Athens Parthenon; the wars of Zeus and the Titans and/or Athena and the Titans in the Pergamum frieze; and the heroic battle scenes in the stone reliefs on the burial casket of Alexander of Macedon. Any survey of the history of Western art is also a review of the history of war, both mythological and historical, as conducted by man - that creature who repeatedly expresses urges of combative aggression, even when brandishing the flag of peace. Such a historical survey brings to mind innumerable masterpieces, like Paulo Uccello's *The Battle of San Romano* (1451-57); Albrecht Altdorfer's *Alexander's Victory* (1529); Nicolas Poussin's *The Destruction of the Temple in Jerusalem* (1625); and other well-known works – reaching their zenith in modern times with Picasso's renowned *Guernica* from 1937.

43 Donald B. Kuspit, "Uncivil War," *Artforum*, April 1983, pp. 34-43.

In 1983, Donald Kuspit published an article titled "Uncivil War."[43] He drew attention to a new, modern perception of the representation of war in twentieth century art – representation characterized by alienation, anonymity, the banality of evil and the totality of destruction. Battle photographs of soldiers bereft of any personal identity – since the Spanish civil war, by way of World War II and onwards – served as the basis for Kuspit's claim regarding the great departure from the traditions of emotional representation that had exalted war to mythological heights, its pinnacle being the Romantic wave of the nineteenth century. Antoine-Jean Gros' giant paintings of *The Battle of Aboukir* (1806) or *The Battle of Eylau* (1808) are two typical examples of an enthusiastic, monumental apotheosis of a hero galloping on his horse and felling victims right and left, echoing the flowering of nationalism and idolation of the hero and heroism in the writings of Friedrich Nietzsche, Thomas Carlyle

"Dispersion," 1994

In November 1994, Kronzon opened the solo exhibition "Dispersion" at Nelly Aman gallery in Tel Aviv (which was to become, over the years, her regular venue). With her unique flair for lingual ambiguity, she chose for the title a Hebrew term denoting simultaneously deployment (as in spatial arrangement, notably in the drawing up of military forces) and slicing or carving (as in the slicing of bread or anything else). Needless to say, the "slicing" aspect charged the installation with a note of violence.

A large number of objects, varying in size from ten to fifty centimeters, were deployed throughout the gallery space; some were cast paper vessels, others found objects rectified by the artist. Previously, in the course of her work with cast paper objects formed in ready-made molds, she had toyed with idea of integrating the replicated castings with their originals – these discarded, damaged, rectified objects. In "Dispersion" she made that transition.

In a text written for the exhibition, she wrote:

> Part of the components of the installation are empty or emptied vessels and unusable containers, part are fragments bearing the memory of the intact whole – two of the principal motifs of the artist's work, generating a reflection of dystopic existence. Each detail of the installation bears a personal declaration facilitating its integral inclusion in the system creating the whole. As it binds together the various limbs of the body of the installation, this set of associations is by nature complex: it possesses a fluid tone of voice, its tempo varies, its language and motifs both personal and collective.[52]

52 From the artist's archive.

Kronzon had been building up the "dispersion" principle since 1992, when she created in her studio an installation of that designation, with objects dispersed on the floor in an anti-structure comprising cast paper containers alongside negatives of cloth dolls, soft rubber molds, plaster casts of foot sections, a military girdle with its buckles painted pink, wax casts of facial parts (of the kind employed in plastic surgery), a roll of iron netting (of the kind used in concrete castings on roads – that is, for construction) upon which

< **Dispersion**, 1994, detail

Dispersion, 1994,
general view   >

the Mishnah and other sources which repeatedly confirm this astounding semantic interpretation, linking birth with burial. It should be added that the artist, who spends most of her time in New York, is well aware of the connection existing in English between "crypt," denoting a grave, and that same term used in the anatomical sense of the expanse of the internal organs.

Ziva Kronzon's work has often been spoken of as the experience of destruction or Holocaust against which the artist grapples with the aid of the forces of order.... Now, that insight requires expansion to the well-worn Jungian affinity between container and womb, and between the fire of destruction and the fire of fecundity, when the apocalypse is channeled into the artist's nightmares as she delves into the archetypal depths of her femininity. In this context, Ziva Kronzon's installations respond to childhood fears to the same extent as they express a mother's dread. Who then is Ziva Kronzon at the level of her terrors: Jephthah's Daughter or Sarah?

*

In 1997, Kronzon exhibited an installation entitled *Personal Shelters* at the Gerhard Marcks Haus in Bremen, Germany. Over twenty containers, battered and scruffy, cylindrical and cubic, all of cast paper painted in metallic and burned hues, were set out in a tight, multi-storied grouping. Objects resembling sacks, barrels, boxes etc., all hollow shells (some without base), were piled up on top of each other, propped up by interior iron rods and merging into a most morbid architectural structure. More than any similarity to personal shelters, this collection of black objects resembled the remains of a village that has been bombed and burned out. Alternately, the "torso" form suggested by some of the objects imposed upon the installment the appearance of a group of terrified refugees huddling together. The vertical iron rods associate the objects with torn, shabby tailor's dummies, bereft of any human identity.

Military Cemetery Plot, detail from the installation **Dispersion**, 1985, plaster, rectified readymade, 29x31x31

Ziva Kronzon at work on **Terra Interdicta II**, 1996

"Terra Interdicta," 1994-2001

The installation *Terra Interdicta* has given Kronzon no rest since it was first exhibited at the Tel Hai sculpture biennial in 1994: set out on the ground inside a military tent (the latter being a curatorial "given" for every installation at the artistic event) was a group of tiny altars/tables, cast in polyester resin as if covered with a white tablecloth, and upon them small black cloth dolls were held tightly by the clamps of booster cables, of the kind used for starting cars or setting off detonations. The installation was also shown that year at the group exhibition "Resist (all) Authority" at Avivson gallery, London. A different version of the installation was displayed at the Yad Labanim museum in Petach Tikva in 1998, as part of a group exhibition entitled "Who are we and where are we headed?" Here Kronzon again set out stages/tables on the floor, this time cast in plaster as if covered with red tablecloths, the jump cables snaking between them, with the "negative" electric clamp grasping the "positive" pole and red lights blinking out warning signals.

Once again, Donald Kuspit composed an essay, dwelling particularly on the "Laocoonian" aspect of her work (that is, the snaking electric cables as an echo of the tormenting serpents in the sculpture *Laocoon*) and regarding the group of square platforms as a unit of soldiers. Here follow the main portions of his text:

> As always with Ziva Kronzon, we are on a memorial battlefield – a kind of treacherous minefield that has been memorized with ironically minimalist intensity. A chaotic scene of conflict and suffering – stress and violence – is presented with vehement understatement and a radical economy of means. The result is what Walter Benjamin calls a "dialectical image" – an image that reconciles contradictory ideas in itself: abstract red squares acquire an anthropomorphic function – eternal geometry becomes subliminally historical. Hypnotically repeated, the squares are so many symbolic, hallucinatory soldiers – or markers for their graves (The lurid red of the squares confirms their transformation into "dragon seeds").
>
> To further complicate the conceptual irony, the squares also represent the mines that killed them, as the booster cables that rest on the squares suggest. The cables

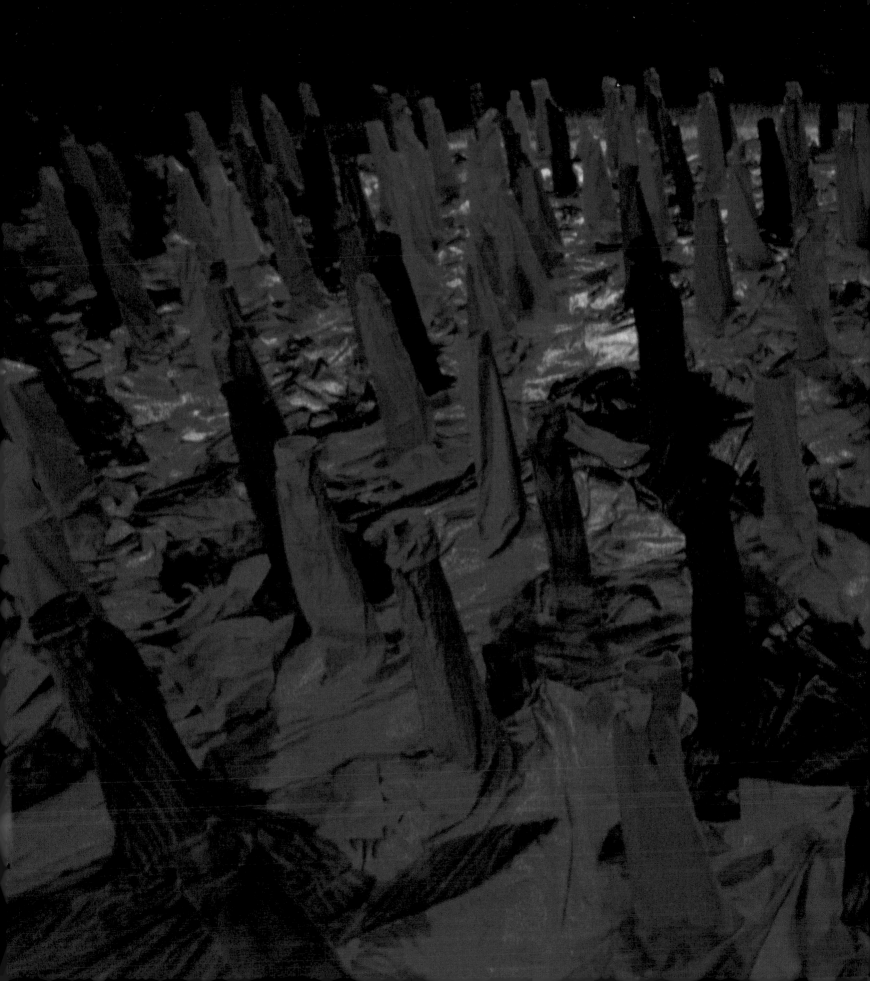

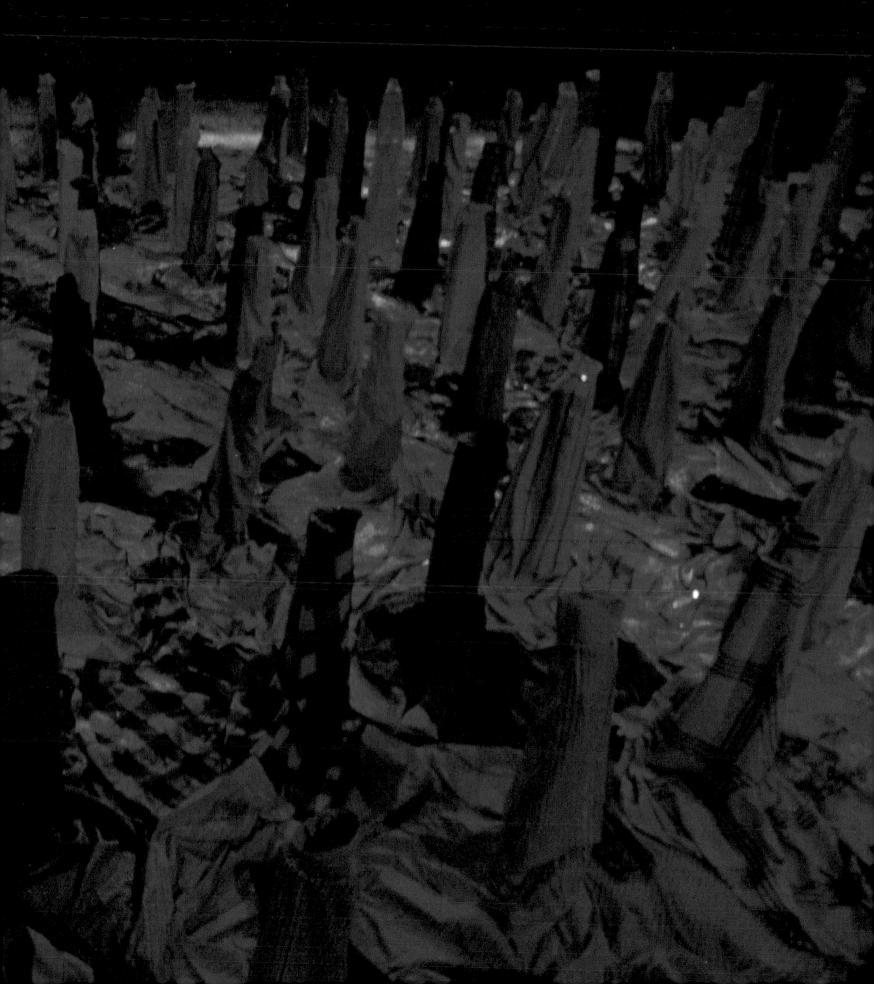

Elegy, 1996, wall installation, mixed media, dimensions variable

Chairs, 1997, color print, 50x70

"Night Vision," 2002

At the end of the nineties and the beginning of the new millennium, Kronzon snapped many photographs of urban ruin, some taken at construction sites. Thus, her photographs were overrun by multitudes of amorphous white stains on the road, or red marks on the road, or windows boarded shut, or a composition of ladders and wooden planks. Wherever she went – New York, Tel Aviv and other cities around the globe – Kronzon repeatedly turned her camera on entropic images.

On the one hand, this development in Kronzon's creativity reflected the great triumph photography had achieved in the global art scene, and particularly in the United States; but on the other hand, Kronzon's photographs constituted a new consistent chapter in the annals of her ongoing preoccupation with printing. Having partially abandoned the "printing" of objects in cast paper and plaster (in favor of resorting to the found objects themselves, albeit in metaphorical composition) – Kronzon turned to photography which enlarges, colors and illuminates the objects, which became the protagonists of a theatrical scene.

In a series commenced as far back as 1993 (!) and exhibited at the Nelly Aman gallery in 1999, Kronzon focused on enlarged photographs of handgun holsters on a white background. Hung in a line, like a mass production assembly line, they continued to owe a debt to the principle of the empty container. The violent association with war, phallic in its similarity to an erection visible through trousers, was now accompanied by a fierce vaginal association, heightening the male-female tension that has consistently marked Kronzon's work. The photographs of the leather holsters with their organic forms were an enlarged version of the original object against a white background, in a repetitive 120x85 cm format. In addition, they resembled relics of inner bodily organs, especially when diverging from the phallic image of the handgun barrel. Their standardized display on the wall transformed the gallery walls into something resembling a sales catalogue of military equipment. At the same time, the seductive sensuality of the soft bulges introduced a contradiction into the lethal objects photographed. Whereas hitherto Kronzon had exhibited the wounded envelope of the acts of killing – the remnants of a ravaged residential

337

area – she now turned to the entire, pristine envelope of the instruments of death themselves, highlighting the chillingly aesthetic-erotic totality of the destructive instruments responsible for the devastation of the intact whole, for the destruction of the aesthetic and the conversion of Eros into Thanatos, death.

It should be noted further that, in another space in the gallery, Kronzon also displayed a long string of photographs of "soldiers" along the upper edge of the walls – a standardized mass replication of lead soldiers from Napoleon's army, printed in negative on a very long canvas strip (creating a ghostly effect). The pseudo-classical frieze "ornamenting" the exhibition walls heightened the aesthetic irony of the lethal weapons (holsters). The series of holster photographs was to be displayed again in April 2002, at the Oscar

Holsters, 1999, Nelly Aman gallery, Tel Aviv

62   Alan G. Artner, "When Subjects Stir Scenarios," *Chicago Tribune*, 26 April 2002.

Friedl gallery in Chicago. In a review of the exhibition, Alan G. Artner, the chief art critic for the *Chicago Tribune*, noted the affinity with the series of handguns that Andy Warhol had painted in his "cold" style, adding: "Will the subject matter disturb an audience familiar with Middle-eastern violence? Will the artist being a woman heighten the deadpan treatment?"[62]

But let us return to the nineties and Kronzon's progressive advance into the medium of photography: as far back as 1994, she pointed her camera at the sight of an abandoned World War II bunker, or a deserted locale that had served as base for a German cannon, or a concrete firing post (on the Normandy coast), etc. In 1995, she created a photographic wall installation, after the manner of Christian Boltanski or Annette Messager, where she hung, pinched by thin wires, approximately fifty photographs of plaster casts of crippled feet, some amputated (ready-made casts, originating in clinics that fit disabled persons with specialized shoes) – like a projection of the "electric" clamps of *Terra Interdicta I* (in itself a kind of "mined" enclosure, anyone venturing into it risking serious injury to his legs) into the photographic domain.

In the years 1998-99, Kronzon photographed a grand chair, shining white against a dark background, and only careful scrutiny can detect the carpenter's clamp grasping its "wounded" legs. At the same time, she photographed blue pipes winding on the ground, and her own red-stained hands handling shredded khaki shirts (in preparation for *Terra Interdicta II*).

In 2000, she photographed dozens of military webbing pouches. These were "neutral," "objective" photographs, identical in size and invariably set against a white background, differences between them restricted to the varying shades of khaki and the changing creases of the closed pouch. In these photographs, Kronzon remained true to the pouch motif we recall as a component of her installations of cast paper containers. In this context, we should also mention two-dimensional paper works dating from 1992, with two black cross-like shapes (the cross shape – a flattened pouch); the hub of each cross is the pouch's front. The cast-paper images transform the pouches into emblems with the presence of a religious Christian sacrificial offering, also bringing to mind the use Josef Beuys made of the cross (in connection with his experience as a wounded World War II fighter pilot, who was rescued by the Red Cross.)

In 2001, Kronzon turned her camera upon a gigantic pile of waste paper she

Granade, 1999, digital print, 40x25

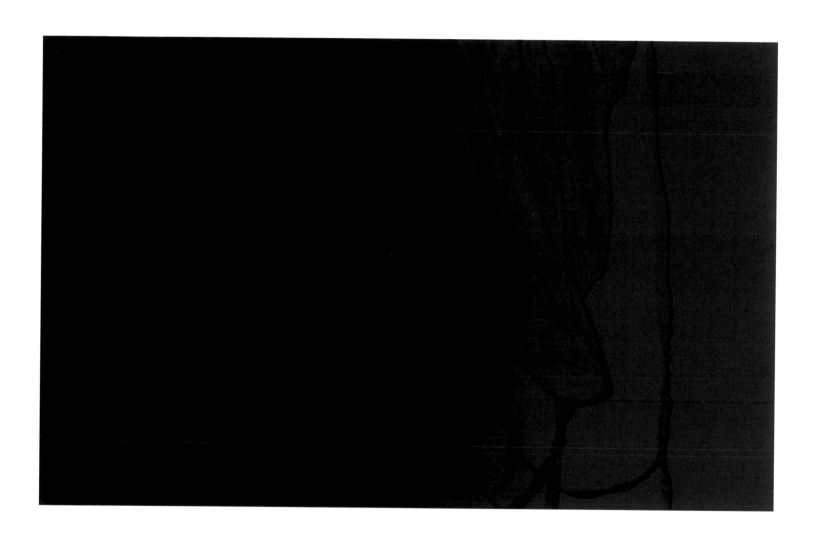

Black Spot (right panel of diptych), 1996-2002, from "Night Vision," color print, 76x100

354   **San Sebastian**, 2006, digital print, 18x35

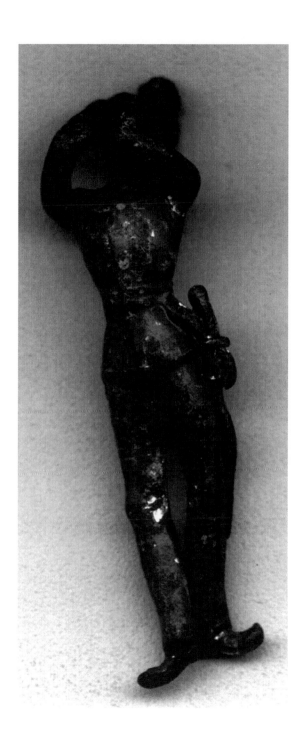

Lead Soldier, 1997-2002, from "Night Vision," computer processing, color print, 1 of 4, 70x29

Discarded Molds, 1998-2002, from "Night Vision," color print, 2 of 13, 90x58 each

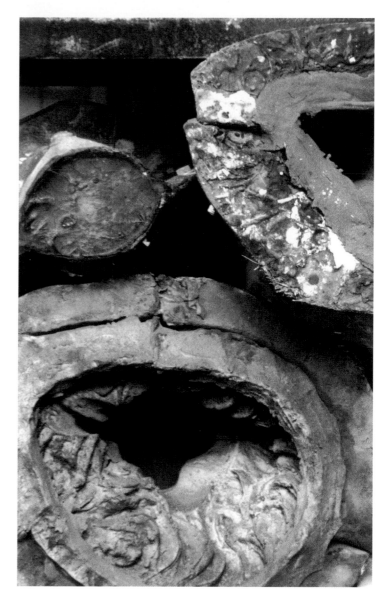

Discarded Molds, 1998-2002, from "Night Vision," color print, 2 of 13, 90x58 each

"Gleaning," 2005

Agnes Varda's documentary film *The Gleaners and I* (*Les Glaneurs et la Glaneuse*) made an enormous impression on Kronzon when she saw it in 2000. Five years later, in the summer of 2005, she presented at the Nelly Aman gallery the exhibition "Gleaning" (its Hebrew title referring to the Biblical injunction directing farmers to leave corners of their fields unharvested, for the benefit of the poor). In the exhibition leaflet it was described thus:

> Gleaning and arranging, memory and forgetfulness, loss and search, illusion and disillusionment, are pairs of words bearing the time dimension, expressing its flow and coming together in Kronzon's artistic language. The installation "Gleaning" is composed of elements she garnered, collected and created in the years 1990-2004. She has welded its parts, taking them apart and putting them back together to create a narrative sequence. The present narrative deals principally with liquids and flowing. "Liquid" [in Hebrew, both noun and verb] is a highly charged and multi-faceted concept. It corresponds with the sets of battered vessels and empty containers – the principal components of her work hitherto – that are witnesses of loss and perhaps, too, expectation of new substance.[65]

65   From the artist's archive.

Kronzon reverted to "archeology," but now the "excavation" of the ancient settlement or home involved a further "excavation" site – her private storeroom. For "Gleaning" is the archeology of the barrow or tumulus of Kronzon's endeavors, just as it uncovers the core of an ancient settlement, howsoever imaginary. A double excavation in time.

Let us commence with "settlement": a spiral system for channeling water that had served some village. as it had been possible in the past to attribute to Kronzon's containers a bygone function of water storage for extinguishing fires, now, apart from cast paper buckets, we observe pipes, drainpipes, funnels – gigantic and small, some inserted into one another to create a "pipe" – channels, furniture etc., some in cast paper, together composing the large spiral of a primitive water channeling system. The system is in ruins, and it is evident to the spectator that the fragments improvised to reconstitute

<   Detail from **Gleaning**, 2005, mixed media, approx. 200x150x70

it have survived severe calamities. The "architectural" improvisations are of a desperate nature: the components, of different height, length and thickness, carry on from one another, snake in and out of one another – most of them in hues of black and rust, all battered and crushed, broken and defeated. A number of wire coils scribble lines in the air, in acknowledgement of their inability to repair the structure as it falls apart. An additional possibility: the desperate attempt at improvisation is by the artist – an "archeologist" or "reconstructor" who does everything to rebuild and secure the supply of water, of salvation, of life.

The spiral structure caves in under its own destruction, capitulating to the environmental chaos in the storeroom's disorganized accumulation of objects (an entropic composition like Josef Beuys' installations, some of which are also "storeroom"-like, such as the permanent exhibit at the Kaiser Wilhelm Museum in Krefeld, Germany). The spiral commences with a group of small lead pipes[66] squeezed into a metal container – possibly a cartridge box, or else a test-tube box (either way, misfortune). Nearby is a wooden box, from which a cast paper container in the familiar black hue rises up, resembling an archaic dolmen-like abstraction of a figure. "Medals" adorn this black, empty object, suggesting the "admiral" or "commander" – the transporter and leader on the course to perdition, whether Charon, the boatman of the dead, or the satanic Aguirre from the eponymous Werner Herzog film. Thus, the spiral form, familiar as a psychoanalytic symbol of the womb as well as symbol of utopian infinity (the Tower of Babel), reverses its identity to emerge as swirling siphon into perdition.

The water channeling system is thus both spiral river and drowning whirlpool. The formal flow of the fragments, not to speak of the virtual flow of the water, affirms the famous Heraclitean adage: "Everything flows"; however, the changing, dynamic water of life turns out to be the water of death, destructive and chilling. The rural structure of life has become a cemetery of human parts and broken objects: two paper casts of feet stumps rest upon a shattered mirror stained with murky liquid (purification water), resting on a stretcher-like structure; a wooden mold contains a plaster death mask; further plaster casts of feet, arms, and other body parts turn the flow into alluvia of chopped-up human remains; A pile of prickly shoe-sole forms completes the

66 In a conversation with the author, Kronzon elaborated on the significance of lead as a symbol of death: the leaden arrow of Thanatos in contrast to the golden arrow of Eros.

Gleaning, 2005, installation, mixed media, dimensions variable, partial view

364 **Gleaning**, 2005, installation, mixed media, dimensions variable, partial view

Gleaning (detail), 2005, mixed media, 25x60x250

Uprooting #1, 2004, digital print, 60x56

Uprooting #2, 2004, digital print, 60x56

Uprooting #3, 2004, digital print, 60x56

Gleaning (detail), 2005, mixed media

Gleaning (detail), 2005, mixed media

Detail from the installation **Dispersion**, 1994, mixed media, 25x35x20

Days of Commemoration, Days of Destruction

A small black-and-white photograph: Dad in khaki uniform and helmet. Photographer unknown. "What the Photograph reproduces to infinity has occurred only once: the Photograph mechanically repeats what could never be repeated existentially."[67] Existentially, Dad can never return again. Never. What remains is the photograph. A small two-dimensional signifier of "that rather terrible thing which is there in every photograph: the return of the dead."[68] But is he who returns, that returning spirit (the *revenant*, to use Derrida's term), identical with the original father, the one and only father known to that young girl Ziva Shisha? "The photograph is the advent of myself as other: a cunning dissociation of consciousness from identity."[69] And in sharper wording: "The photograph...represents that very subtle moment when...I experience a micro-version of death (of parenthesis): I am truly becoming a specter."[70] And also: "When I discover myself in the product of this operation [that is, photography. G.O.] what I see is that I have become Total Image, which is to say, Death in person; others...turn me, ferociously, into an object,"[71] and thus "ultimately, what I am seeking in the photograph taken of me...is Death: Death is the *eidos* of that photograph."[72]

Returning to Dad, bringing Dad back, descending into the world of the dead and emerging with him – the well-known mythological tale, whose outcome is equally familiar. A journey from a faded black-and-white signifier to the signified in dark black; each exhibition by Kronzon entails embarking anew on such a voyage. To her, each exhibition is a rite for the evocation of a spirit, like a commemorative candle on Memorial Day, for the objects on display resemble a "monument" – or rather, an "anti-monument," which essentially belongs somewhere between tombstones and fine art sculptures: "The tomb draws us to the world of death, the sculpture to non-life at the cultural level, the monument is the encounter between the living and the dead at the level of Nature."[73]

Kronzon's anti-monumental sculptures have internalized the monument's awareness only in order to smash it. In her objects we identify equally the particular signification of gravestones, the universal symbolism of art, and

67 Roland Barthes, *Camera Lucida: Reflections on Photography*, trans. Richard Howard, The Noonday Press, New York, 1988, p. 4.

68 *Ibid.*, p. 9.

69 *Ibid.*, p. 12.

70 *Ibid.*, p. 14.

71 *Ibid.*, p. 14.

72 *Ibid.*, p. 15.

73 Gideon Ofrat, "The Aesthetics of the Monument," in *The Artistic Medium*, Stavit, Tel Aviv, 1987, p. 47 (first published in *Kav* no. 4-5, November 1982, pp. 58-62) [Hebrew].

the iconicism of the monument (which is the presence of the symbolized as a symbol): for example, just as the iconicism of the Tel Hai lion monument (for those who died in the 1920 battle over the Tel Hai settlement) asserts that the dead resemble lions, a field of red shirt sleeves proclaims a bloody battlefield. But at this semiotic level Kronzon's work is unique: from her point of view, each of her exhibitions (and possibly, each object) is like a gravestone signifying a specific dead person – her father. However, in the transition of her creative work from sign to symbol she ascends from the personal to the general, from gravestone and monument to artistic creation; she advances from the artist's private case to the human experience of the entire audience, just as she breaks free of signifying a particular location – from the "here lies" or "here took place" signification of the monument or gravestone (and for Kronzon, every exhibition proclaims, first and foremost, the destruction of a particular house, her childhood home back in Kiryat Haim) to a work that symbolizes every place – hence too the possibility of exhibiting it anywhere, whether in Israel, America, or Germany.[74]

The message symbolized by the monument specifies a time and an event: at this or that place, a terrible (or sublime) event occurred; remember that event. Accordingly, Kronzon's anti-monuments construct an ostensibly concrete location – the site of a demolished house where that event occured. However, whereas the space of the monument is dependent upon ceremonial times – such as Memorial Day – Kronzon's sculptures do not depend upon "monument time" (which is that special time when monuments are charged with a mythological power, when the encounter between the living and the dead takes place); for as artworks, her sculptures are supposed to work at all times, and by virtue of their "artistic summons" they do not enjoin us to accept the world of myth (as monuments do). At most, they bear a recommendation to learn a lesson. Of course, these sculptures do not enfold the idealistic drama of the monument – heroism, self-sacrifice etc.; nor are they a symbol of the victim's exemplary heroism. "The domain of the monument is a purely ideal domain. The monument is forever positive. The monument is never complex, certainly not dialectical."[75] Not so Kronzon's anti-monuments: they are "negative" in their focus on the aspect of destruction and perdition, and they are dialectical. It is not into a world of strength that they introduce us, but

74 On the ostensible tension between monuments and fine art works, particularly avant-garde ones, see *Ibid.*, pp. 48–51.

75 *Ibid.*, p. 49.

374

Surrogate Family, 1990-2006, digital print, 25x40

sculptures respond to the power and solid uniformity of the monument with soft disintegrating and decaying vulnerability. And while the four elements that are frequently at work in monuments – earth, air, fire and water – can also be discerned obliquely in Kronzon's sculptures, she does not seek the eternal flame of the psychic symbol, and refers to the fire of destruction instead; and unlike the "living" water gurgling in many monuments, in Kronzon's works water is present through an association to fire-extinguishing vessels; the soil of the monument (the soil that gives birth and buries, embodied in monumental rocks) has been transformed in Kronzon's works to the simulative appearance of iron; and air (such as the breeze that blows through Dani Karavan's *Negev Monument*, Beersheba, 1963-68) is manifested in the emptiness of her vessels.

From all these aspects, then, Kronzon reverses monument values. Each new exhibition of hers is a renewed effort, and an additional failure, in the attempt at a "mythical" encounter, which is also an attempt to reconstitute the shattered past. The memory guiding her is the memory of an inaccessible absence, and consequently she is doomed to theatrical cycles of memory, to "general rehearsals" of sorts for a play entitled "A Playwright in Search of a Single Character"[82] – and between one performance and the next, every pile of stones, every pile of remnants, bears a memory.

82 Paraphrasing the title of Pirendello's *Six Characters in Search of an Author.*

Stereoicon, 2006, digital print, 18x33

Triage (Salvaged Church Stones, Dresden), 1994-2006, digital print, 29x70

379

Downcast Eyes, 2004, digital print, 80x52 each

To Date

Untitled, 2001-2, Xerox print, 28x20; created following an "open call" for artists' reactions to 9/11 events. Acquired and exhibited by the Library of Congress in Washington DC.

In 2005, Kronzon held a solo exhibition at Makor – a Jewish cultural center in north-west Manhattan. In the spirit of a return to the storeroom or self-archeology in her studio, Kronzon returned to her past works – displaying the installation *Personal Shelters* from 1997 (see above), hanging blackened cast-paper vessels on the wall, creating a variation on the reddened shirts we recall from *Terra Interdicta II*, and re-fashioning the "baby stroller" installation from her previous exhibition, with the embalmed frogs they carried replaced by two cylindrical unpolished wood beams (of the kind peasants use in constructing their shacks) which were placed on the strollers: yet another house destroyed/rebuilt in Kronzon's ongoing saga.

Kronzon continues to delve into and "organize life" as she puts it. At the moment, she is preoccupied with internal rummaging in the photographed materials accumulated in her "archive" over the course of many years, which had served, as we recall, in her 2002 "Night Vision." She continues to "arrange" her studio, uncovering old materials, modifying previous works, categorizing (to a considerable degree, this present volume would not have been possible without this self-cataloguing) – recycling more and more materials and objects in new combinations and structures for the exhibitions she has put on over past years.

She is already planning her coming steps: "I have at home old-new photographic works, an extension of 'Night Vision.'" Furthermore, she plans to return to drawing, the medium in which she specialized and excelled at the outset of her career. And while it is evident that in this work she will continue to deal with the mutual sufferings inflicted in war – her constant theme – she senses that she is on the verge of a dramatic turnabout: "It's like starting over, and I'm going to do it. On a smaller or larger scale. It seems to me that I'm on the verge of a new phase in my artistic work, and I don't know where I'll find myself. That's my plan for the future." There we have it, a plan without plan.

*

As these lines were being written, northern Israel was taking the impact of thousands of missiles fired off in a bloody war with Hizbullah, the Lebanese Shiite militia. Approximately a million Israeli refugees fled southwards, just as a million Lebanese civilians escaped to the north. Israeli airforce planes relentlessly pounded Lebanon's cities, towns and villages. Babies, women, old people and soldiers were killed on both sides of the border, and many more suffered terrible wounds. "To my regret, my works are forever relevant," Kronzon says with a wry smile.

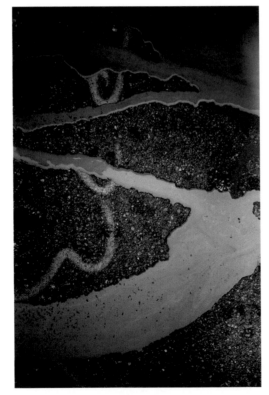

Downcast Eyes, 2004, digital print, 80x52 each

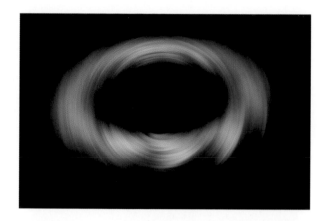

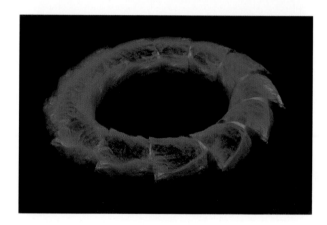

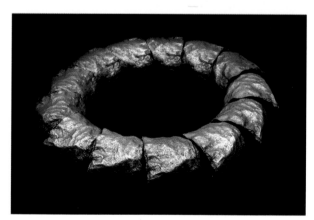

Entropy, 1990-2006, digital print, 90x30

Downcast Eyes, 2004, digital print, 60x91

Downcast Eyes, 2004, digital print, 60x91

Downcast Eyes (diptych), 2004, digital print, 80x108

Downcast Eyes (diptych), 2004, digital print, 80x108

Ziva Kronzon, drawing by Shira
Kronzon, 1985

1991	– One-person show, Herzliya Museum of Contemporary Art, Israel
	– One-person show, Doris Wallkopf gallery, Darmstadt, Germany
	– One-person show, Lupfert gallery, Hanover, Germany
	– Participates in the exhibition "Chords and Discords," Hudson River Museum, New York
	– Participates in group exhibition, Josh Baer gallery, New York
	– Participates in "Paper Works by Five," Hammond Museum, New York
1992	– One-person show, "Close Formation," Bertha Urdang gallery, New York
	– One-person show, Nelly Aman gallery, Tel Aviv
	– Participates in the exhibition "Drawings and Prints," Hammond Museum, New York
	– One-person show, East End Arts Council, New York
	– One-person show, Doris Wallkopf gallery, Darmstadt, Germany
1993	– One-person show, Avivson gallery, London
	– Participates in group exhibition, Brownson gallery, Manhattanville College, New York
	– Participates in group exhibition, Doris Wallkopf gallery, Darmstadt, Germany
	– Participates in group exhibition, Neuer Kunstverein, Aschaffenburg, Germany
1994	– One-person show, "Dispersion," Nelly Aman gallery, Tel Aviv
	– Participates in "Tel Hai Events '94," sculpture biennial, Israel
	– Participates in the exhibition "Resist (all) Authority," Avivson gallery, London
	– Participates in the exhibition "Sketches and Prints," Doris Wallkopf gallery, Darmstadt, Germany
1995	– One-person show, Nelly Aman gallery, Tel Aviv
	– Participates in group exhibition of sketches, Doris Wallkopf gallery, Darmstadt, Germany
	– One-person show, Tova Ossman gallery, Tel Aviv
	– Participates in the exhibition "The Dimension of Paper," Daphna Naor gallery, Jerusalem
1996	– One-person show, Blanis Museum of Fine Arts, Montovideo, Uruguay
	– Participates in group exhibition, Hudson River Museum, New York
	– One-person show, Ashdod Museum, Israel
	– Participates in the exhibition "Charles Darwin," Art Now gallery, London
	– Participates in the exhibition "Paper in disguise," Dieu Donné Papermill, New York
	– Participates in group exhibition, Lehman College Art Gallery, Bronx, New York
	– Participates in the exhibition "Peace," Eretz Israel Museum, Tel Aviv
1997	– One-person show, "Personal Shelters," Gerhard Marx House, Bremen, Germany
	– Participates in the exhibition "Co-Op," Eretz Israel Museum, Tel Aviv
	– Participates in the exhibition "MiniArtura," Palazzo Ducale, Gubbio, Italy
	– Participates in the exhibition "Works in Paper," Landesmuseum, Linz, Austria
1998	– One-person show, "Who are we and where are we headed?" Yad Labanim museum, Petach Tikva
	– One-person show, "Terra Interdicta II," Zapata Art and Culture gallery, Stuttgart, Germany
	– Participates in the exhibition "Paper–Value–Paper," Museum of Modern Art, Ramat Gan
	– Participates in group exhibition, Lindenberg gallery, New York
1999	– Participates in group exhibition, Nelly Aman gallery, Tel Aviv
	– Participates in group exhibition, Ashdod Museum, Israel
2000	– Participates in the exhibition "Over Fifty Years," Landesmuseum, Linz, Austria
	– One-person show, Avivson gallery, Paris, France

Ziva Kronzon, drawing by Iris
Kronzon, 1982

	– One-person show, "Terra Interdicta II," Impavillon Kulturzentrum, Wells, Austria
	– Participates in the exhibition "Small Works," New York University Art Gallery, New York
2001	– One-person show, "Terra Interdicta II," Artists House, Tel Aviv
	– Participates in the exhibition "Breaking the Rules," Katonah Museum of Art, Katonah, New York
	– Participates in the exhibition "Hands," The Israel Museum (Youth Section), Jerusalem
	– Participates in the exhibition "Art America-Israel," Habima gallery, Tel Aviv
2002	– One-person show, Oskar Friedl gallery, Chicago
	– One-person show, "Night Vision," Nelly Aman gallery, Tel Aviv
	– Participates in group exhibition, Fulton Street gallery, Troy, New York
	– Participates in the exhibition "Works on Paper," Oskar Friedl gallery, Chicago
2003	– One-person show, Ritmogram, Bad Ischl, Austria
	– Participates in the exhibition "Commemoration – 9/11," Library of Congress, Washington DC
	– Participates in the exhibition "Fabrication," Ashdod Museum, Israel
	– Participates in the exhibition "From thy Ruins I shall Build thee," Time for Art Gallery, Tel Aviv
2004	– One-person show, Zapata Art and Culture gallery, Stuttgart, Germany
	– Participates in the exhibition "The Puppet Show," Time for Art Gallery, Tel Aviv
2005	– One-person show, "Gleaning," Nelly Aman gallery, Tel Aviv
	– Participates in the exhibition "The Ephemeral Alteration of Being," Makor, New York
	– Participates in group exhibition, Oskar Friedl gallery, Chicago
	Participates in the exhibition "The Egg," Ashdod Museum, Israel
	– Participates in the exhibition "Divine in. tent – Markers VI," The Artist's Museum, Venice
2007	– One-person show, "Works on Paper," Nelly Aman gallery, Tel Aviv
	– Retrospective one-person show, Zhou B Art Center, Chicago

Collections

Library of Congress, Washington DC, USA
Landesmuseum, Linz, Austria
Sprengel Museum, Hannover, Germany
Herbert F. Johnson Museum of Art, Cornell University, New York, USA
The Israel museum, Jerusalem, Israel
National Museum of Women in the Arts, Washington DC, USA
Herzliya Museum of Contemporary Art, Herzliya, Israel
Ashdod Museum of Art, Ashdod, Israel
Bezalel Academy of Art and Design, Jerusalem, Israel
Art Students League of New York, New York, USA
Private collections in Israel, the USA and Germany

Trousseau, 2007, digital print,
30x17.5